RECRUITING and FORMING YOUR PARISH INITIATION TEAM

DONNA M. ESCHENAUER

LTP
LITURGY
TRAINING
PUBLICATIONS

Nihil Obstat
Rev. Mr. Daniel G. Welter, JD
Chancellor
Archdiocese of Chicago
April 21, 2021

Imprimatur
Most Rev. Robert G. Casey
Vicar General
Archdiocese of Chicago
April 21, 2021

The *Nihil Obstat* and *Imprimatur* are declarations that the material is free from doctrinal or moral error, and thus is granted permission to publish in accordance with c. 827. No legal responsibility is assumed by the grant of this permission. No implication is contained herein that those who have granted the *Nihil Obstat* and *Imprimatur* agree with the content, opinions, or statements expressed.

This book was edited by Timothy A. Johnston. Michael A. Dodd was the production editor, Anna Manhart was the designer, and Juan Alberto Castillo was the production artist.

Cover art: Shutterstock/sachch /Gaianami Design /Kwitka

25 24 23 22 21 1 2 3 4 5

Printed in the United States of America

Library of Congress Control Number: 2021931718

ISBN: 978-1-61671-601-1

RFPI

Contents

Preface

Karen Hinman's book *How to Form a Catechumenate Team* was published in 1986. At the time, it was an essential tool for those who braved the new territory of initiation ministry. My personal copy (which I still own) is well marked, highlighted, and filled with handwritten notes in the margins. As a new coordinator of initiation ministry, I read and reread Hinman's book so that I could appropriately form a catechumenate team and strive for full implementation of the *Rite of Christian Initiation of Adults* in my parish. Without a doubt, Hinman's book was a jewel for its time! It is my sincere hope that *Recruiting and Forming Your Parish Initiation Team* will serve your parish in a similar way, giving well-defined understanding and direction on how to recruit, develop, and form a team of ministers for appropriate and full implementation of the *Rite of Christian Initiation of Adults*.

In *The Role of the Coordinator in Christian Initiation: A Pastoral and Practical Guide*, I begin with a story of how I became acquainted with the *Rite of Christian Initiation of Adults*. After being a sponsor for my neighbor, I was invited to serve on the initiation team as the coordinator of the sponsors. My personal experience of being a team member was like nothing I had ever experienced before. I eagerly looked forward to our monthly team meetings because, in addition to training and discussion, Scripture, prayer, and reflection were an important part of every agenda. I always left team meetings with a deeper experience of God, a richer understanding of the Church, a profound appreciation for the sacraments in my own life, and a joyful enthusiasm for being a part of my parish community.

This book is meant to help the reader provide a similar experience for the parish's initiation team.

The information I present in this book flows, first, from my love for the *Rite of Christian Initiation of Adults*, as well as from over thirty years of pastoral experience as a sponsor, catechist, and coordinator. When the 1988 edition of the rite was promulgated, I had the opportunity to train initiation ministers for my home diocese. I never lost my fervor for the rite, and it is woven into all of my research and writing. I now have the opportunity to teach graduate courses on the rite to future priests and lay ministers who are called to service in the Church.

I consider initiation ministry to be a sacred trust. That being said, it is my sincere desire to add my voice to the various models for the practice of initiation ministry. In addition, it is my confident expectation that readers of this book will catch my enthusiasm for a ministry that holds within it the potential to transform an entire parish, a ministry that invites us to care for those people, who, touched by the Holy Spirit, heroically knock on our door.

This book is written for coordinators of Christian initiation as well as for priests, catechists, sponsors, and all who are dedicated to a team and collegial approach to ministry. For those involved in initiation ministry nothing replaces reading and rereading the ritual text of the *Rite of Christian Initiation of Adults*. A systematic understanding of the rite leads to good pastoral practice. In addition, commentaries, such as this book, also support an understanding for good practice. In many ways, this book flows from the wisdom found in other books—for example, my own work, *The Role of the Coordinator in Christian Initiation*; *The Role of the Priest in Christian Initiation* by Stephen S. Wilbricht; *Preaching for Discipleship: Preparing Homilies for Christian Initiation* by Michael Connors; and Ronald Lewinski's *An Introduction to the RCIA: The Vision of Christian Initiation*. In addition, Michael Ruzicki's *Guide for Training Initiation Ministers: An Introduction to the RCIA*; and *Guide for Celebrating Christian Initiation with Adults* by Victoria Tufano, Paul Turner, and D. Todd Williamson. These are all are valuable resources for initiation team formation.

For me, writing a book is another way of teaching. In addition to the action and presence of God in my life, I would not have the ability to do this without the gifted teachers, dedicated mentors, enthusiastic students, supportive colleagues, and faith-filled spiritual advisors that I have encountered along my own faith journey.

I am deeply grateful to the editors at Liturgy Training Publications for inviting me to write this book. I am humbled by their trust, not only in my ability to present this valuable information, but also for their recognition of my love for the *Rite of Christian Initiation of Adults*. I especially want to thank Timothy Johnston for his support and editorial guidance from the time this book was merely an idea.

This book could not have been written in such a timely way if it were not for my colleagues at St. Joseph's Seminary and College, especially Msgr. Peter Vaccari, Fr. Kevin O'Reilly, and Dean Christine Hammill-Cregan. I have been granted a sabbatical, which gave me the luxury of making the writing of this book a priority. I am deeply indebted to the help of Cynthia Harrison and Roenice Gonzalez, who kindly followed up on many of the administrative details in my absence.

Most of my writing was done in the serene, grace-filled atmosphere of the Seminary of the Immaculate Conception in Huntington, Long Island, New York. I wish to thank Msgr. Charles Fink and Linda Zollo for their wonderful hospitality. Elyse Hayes and the library staff provided me with a conducive environment for writing as well as a wealth of resources. In addition, I am sincerely grateful to the Missionaries of the Most Holy Eucharist, who reside at the seminary, for providing a peaceful space for retreat, silence, and prayer.

I am always indebted to my family's endless support, especially my husband Paul. His complete recognition of the time and effort it takes to write is deeply appreciated. Finally, I want to thank you, the readers of this book. It is my sincere hope that this work will guide you toward an enthusiastic implementation of the *Rite of Christian Initiation of Adults*, particularly in regard to forming an initiation team. I dedicate this work to the honor and glory of God. "Rejoice in the Lord always; again I will say, Rejoice!" (Philippians 4:4).

Gaudete Sunday—Third Sunday of Advent
December 15, 2019

Introduction

Christians are known as people of words: they have a story to tell about how God has given eternal life to humans and a doctrine about the meaning of the story. And when they gather to celebrate the life they live and the story they tell, they practice rites.[1]

The *Rite of Christian Initiation of Adults* is a rite of the Church brilliantly designed to tell the Christian story to those seeking Christ in and through the Roman Catholic Church. The *Rite of Christian Initiation of Adults* tells the story through a process of distinct periods and ritual steps. The rite takes those seeking Christ on a spiritual journey, a journey that no one has to travel alone. In the early Church, when a person wanted to become a Christian they went and lived in the Christian community so that they could learn from the Christian's daily way of life. In much the same way, the expectation expressed in the *Rite of Christian Initiation of Adults* is that the entire parish community travels the journey with inquirers, catechumens, candidates, the elect, and neophytes through prayer, support, and, very important, witness. Significantly, paragraph 9 of the introduction to the *Rite of Christian Initiation of Adults* states that "the initiation of adults is the responsibility of all the baptized. Therefore, the community must always be fully prepared in the pursuit of its apostolic vocation to give help to those who are searching for Christ." This being said, ideally, on behalf of the parish community, an initiation team should

1. Liam G. Walsh, OP, *Sacraments of Initiation: A Theology of Rite, Word, and Life* (Chicago: Liturgy Training Publications, 2011), xiii.

be developed and formed to intimately walk the journey and faithfully tell the story to those who come with an open heart seeking initiation into the Church.

In light of Liam Walsh's insight, *Recruiting and Forming Your Parish Initiation Team* is about a team approach to initiation ministry. It provides information on how to recruit, develop, and form an initiation team that will accompany inquirers, catechumens, candidates, the elect, and neophytes on their spiritual journey. It is about how to train an initiation team to tell the Christian story in a way that will set hearts on fire for Jesus Christ and, at the same time, give them a profound sense of belonging to a supportive, life-giving parish community. In sum, this book attempts not only to lay out a plan on how to develop and form the initiation team to tell the story in a way that will move the newcomer toward humble prayer, reverent worship, and dynamic mission but also to provide the necessary background for what it means to be engaged in the practice of ministry.

It should be noted that the rite never mentions a coordinator or an initiation team. Without a team, however, initiation ministry can be overwhelming. Therefore, a knowledgeable and dedicated team, under the guidance of a well-informed coordinator, is key to full and appropriate implementation of the rite. Full implementation of the rite demonstrates loving care for those who come seeking initiation into the Church and, at the same time, holds the potential to revitalize your parish community into becoming an evangelizing parish. The chapters of this book are intended to guide the reader to this end. What follows is meant to be straightforward. It presumes a basic familiarity with the RCIA ritual text, and references to the text will be made throughout the book as needed.

The design of this book is very much like a workshop or seminar. It is meant to be conversational in tone, and the chapters build on each other. Therefore, it is best to read the chapters in order. I hope that each chapter will teach, affirm, and enlighten you. My ultimate goal is to spark greater enthusiasm for initiation ministry and reinforce the vision that a team approach is the best way to engage the parish in the process of Christian initiation.

The first three chapters of this book provide essential background for better appreciation of the focus of this book—recruiting and forming your parish's initiation team. Chapter 1 provides an overview of the vision of the *Rite of Christian Initiation of Adults* (RCIA), which is the context for forming a team. It looks at the RCIA as a "living ritual" and emphasizes the appropriate language we should use to give it meaning. In addition, the chapter explores how and why the RCIA was restored following the Second Vatican Council, which gives impetus to appropriate and full implementation of the rite. Chapter 2 looks at the practice of ministry in general. It explores the rationale for ministry found in Sacred Scripture and Church documents. Flowing from this, the central ministerial features of discipleship, vocation, and discernment are discussed. Chapter 3 examines the classic dimensions of ministry formation, which includes human formation, spiritual formation, pastoral formation, and intellectual formation.

Chapter 4 focuses more specifically on the practice of initiation ministry. The chapter looks at the essence of initiation ministry that is rooted in a liturgical spirituality and places greater awareness of the meaning of the sacraments of initiation in the life of the team member. It also highlights the role of the coordinator and how a coordinator can best work with the initiation team and collaborate with the pastor, priests, deacons, musicians, and other leaders of ministry that are relevant to the implementation of the *Rite of Christian Initiation of Adults*. Chapter 5 looks at the importance of the role of the parish community in relationship to the initiation team. Chapter 6 looks at team recruitment and the ideal vision for a year-round catechumenate. The elements of this chapter are key to avoiding ministry burnout! The various aspects of developing a team are explored in chapter 7, from developing a new team to working with and enhancing an existing team. Chapter 8 looks at how to form and train sponsors, hospitality ministers, facilitators for dismissal catechesis, and catechists for extended catechesis. Finally, an appendix includes sample team meetings, a guide for team formation for coordinators, a model for celebrating the dismissal on Sunday, and resources to guide you in your ministry.

Outline for Christian Initiation of Adults

Second Step

Election or Enrollment of Names

This is the liturgical rite, usually celebrated on the First Sunday of Lent, by which the Church formally ratifies the catechumens' readiness for the sacraments of initiation and the catechumens, now the elect, express the will to receive these sacraments.

Period of the Catechumenate

This is the time, in duration corresponding to the progress of the individual, for the nurturing and growth of the catechumens' faith and conversion to God; celebrations of the word and prayers of exorcisms and blessing are meant to assist the process.

First Step

Acceptance Into the Order of Catechumens

This is the liturgical rite, usually celebrated on some annual date or dates, marking the beginning of the catechumenate proper, as the candidates express and the Church accepts their intention to respond to God's call to follow the way of Christ.

Period of Postbaptismal Catechesis or Mystagogy

This is the time, usually the Easter season, following the celebration of initiation, during which the newly initiated experience being fully a part of the Christian community by means of pertinent catechesis and particularly by participation with all the faithful in the Sunday eucharistic celebration.

Third Step

Celebration of the Sacraments of Initiation

This is the liturgical rite, usually integrated into the Easter Vigil, by which the elect are initiated through baptism, confirmation, and the eucharist.

Period of Purification and Enlightenment

This is the time immediately preceding the elects' initiation, usually the Lenten season preceding the celebration of this initiation at the Easter Vigil; it is a time of reflection, intensely centered on conversion, marked by celebration of the scrutinies and presentations and the preparation rites on Holy Saturday.

Period of Evangelization and Precatechumenate

This is a time, of no fixed duration or structure, for inquiry and introduction to Gospel values, an opportunity for the beginnings of faith.

Abbreviations

AG: *Ad gentes* (Decree on the Church's Missionary Activity)

CCC: *Catechism of the Catholic Church*

CD: *Christus Dominus* (Decree on the Pastoral Office of Bishops in the Church)

CIC: *Codex iuris canonici* (Code of Canon Law)

CL: *Christifideles laici* (On the Vocation and the Mission of the Faithful in the Church and in the Modern World)

EG: *Evangelii gaudium* (The Joy of the Gospel)

GE: *Gaudete et exsultate* (On the Call to Holiness)

GIRM: *General Instruction of the Roman Missal*

LG: *Lumen gentium* (Dogmatic Constitution on the Church)

NDC: *National Directory for Catechesis*

NS: *National Statues for the Catechumenate*

OC: *Order of Confirmation*

RCIA: *Rite of Christian Initiation of Adults*

SC: *Sacrosanctum concilium* (Constitution on the Sacred Liturgy)

CHAPTER ONE

A Living Ritual

The *Rite of Christian Initiation Adults* (RCIA) is rooted in the New Testament and in the early tradition of the Christian community. As St. Paul reminds the Romans, "We were indeed buried with him through baptism into death, so that, just as Christ was raised from the dead by the glory of the Father, we too might live in the newness of life" (Romans 6:4). And the Acts of the Apostles speaks about Peter and the administration of baptism (2:41; 10:1–11, 18). Acts reveals the stories of faith and shows us that people in the Apostolic Church went through several stages toward baptism. The RCIA as we know it today is an adaptation of the rites from the early Church and consists of four periods and three ritual steps, as shown on the preceding page's outline of Christian initiation.

Since the early centuries of the Church there have been many twists and turns in the process of Christian initiation that are beyond the scope of this book.[1] What is important for our understanding is that the *Rite of Christian Initiation of Adults* has been rediscovered and reclaimed in modern times and remains responsive to the Gospel mandate, "Go, therefore, and make disciples of all nations, baptizing them in the name of the Father, and of the Son, and of the holy Spirit, teaching them to observe all that I have commanded you" (Matthew 28:19–20). It is equally important to see that the *Rite of Christian Initiation of Adults* presents a renewed appreciation for the nature of conversion and the stages of faith development and, very significantly, highlights that Christianity is a way of living in the world. Moreover, the rite upholds a restored vision of the mission and nature of the Church. It also gives flesh to how the sacraments of initiation call us to carry out this mission.

1. See Paul Turner, *The Hallelujah Highway: A History of the Catechumenate* (Chicago: Liturgy Training Publications, 2000) and Edward Yarnold, SJ, *The Awe-Inspiring Rites of Initiation: The Origins of the RCIA* (Collegeville, MN: Liturgical Press, 1994).

RCIA: A Ritual Process, Not a Program

We have all have heard the old adage that Christian initiation is "a process and not a program." While there is truth to this statement, I would like to emphasize that RCIA is more. It is a rite, a ritual process that welcomes, forms, and initiates new members in and through a series of periods and steps that take place over a period of time. In *An Introduction to the RCIA: The Vision of Christian Initiation*, Ronald Lewinski affirms, "We have learned not to approach the rite as a 'program' but as a living ritual that is capable of pastoral adaptation and is respectful of the individual."[2] But have we? In many cases, a common misunderstanding prevails regarding the very essence of the *Rite of Christian Initiation of Adults*. An examination of many parish bulletins and websites shows reference to the "RCIA Program." It is my sincere hope that the readers of this book will work to change this misunderstanding.

As someone steeped in pastoral ministry, I am well aware of the reality that many parishes operate with small staffs where everyone has a tremendous workload. In many cases, the ideal of a collaborative pastoral team consisting of priests, deacons, and professionally educated full-time lay ecclesial ministers is far from a reality. In many dioceses, parishes are merging, and the priest and the staff are stretched between multiple congregations. Even when parishes are not merged, the pastor often works alone and, due to financial strain, depends greatly on volunteers to fill various positions. Sadly, this often results in a maintenance mode of operation. One consequence of this is that the *Rite of Christian Initiation of Adults* becomes a series of classes that takes place over a school-year calendar. Minimizing the rich potential of the RCIA compromises the evangelizing character of the Church. And, as we are all very aware, the ministry of evangelization—the proclamation of the life, death, and resurrection of Jesus Christ—is vital to the health and well-being of parish life today and in the future.

Out of sheer love for the Church and its mission, I would like to emphasize how crucial it is to understand that the RCIA is *not* a program. Initiation ministers need to make a concerted effort to use language that is appropriate to this ministry. Words matter! Words give meaning to

2. Lewinski, *An Introduction to the RCIA*, vii.

what we do. Therefore, it is vitally important to recognize the *Rite of Christian Initiation of Adults* for exactly what it is—a rite: a ritual process for those, "who after hearing the mystery of Christ proclaimed, consciously and freely seek the living God and enter a way of faith and conversion as the Holy Spirit opens their hearts" (RCIA, 1). As Lewinski profoundly states, it is a "living ritual." Once we understand the Church's vision for RCIA, we can be intentional about how we speak about this rite. This understanding of the Church's vision will come across to others in and through the words that we use to speak or write about it. For example, as we look to describe what initiation ministers actually do, we would say, "The coordinator and team participate in the initiation ministry of the Church or catechumenal ministry." In my experience, I often hear people say, "I teach RCIA." This is not an accurate way to articulate the ministry of the catechist. Rather, initiation ministers should get used to saying, "I am a catechist for the catechumenate." We can help others become accustomed to the appropriate language when we use it consistently in our team meetings, with our participants, with the parish community, and through bulletin articles, websites, and social media.

Specifically, the *Rite of Christian Initiation of Adults* is the official rite of the Church used for the initiation of adults not baptized as infants (RCIA, part 1) or for those validly baptized in another ecclesial community who desire to enter into the full communion of the Catholic Church (RCIA, part 2). It important to remember that "adult" also refers to children of catechetical age who were not baptized in the Catholic Church as infants or those children baptized in another ecclesial community seeking full communion of the Catholic Church (part 2).[3]

Labeling RCIA as a parish program may come from the fact that one aspect of this ritual process is catechesis. Regarding catechesis, we are very familiar with a long history of a program model with a distinct set of lessons set to a fixed calendar, usually an academic calendar. Once we understand catechesis within the context of the RCIA, however, catechetical leaders can better grasp what the *National Directory for Catechesis* (NDC) uncompromisingly proclaims: "The implementation of the *Rite of Christian Initiation of Adults* in many dioceses and parishes in the United

3. See Rita Burns Senseman, Victoria M. Tufano, Paul Turner, and D. Todd Williamson, *Guide for Celebrating Christian Initiation with Children* (Chicago: Liturgy Training Publications, 2017).

States has emphasized the need for a catechesis based more directly on the baptismal catechumenate" (NDC, p. 10).[4] In other words, the NDC calls us to understand catechesis as a process that is fully engaged in the liturgical year, community, liturgical rites, and apostolic works (RCIA, 75). In the end, this understanding of catechesis beckons a lifelong journey of mystagogy for children, youth, young adults, and adults.

RCIA: Liturgy That Engages Catechesis

While the entire *Rite of Christian Initiation of Adults* is formative, the Period of the Catechumenate (RCIA, 75–117) is specifically the time for catechesis. A rite that includes catechesis—this is significant! This is what makes the RCIA unique. It is liturgy—a liturgy that takes place over a period of time, and it is a liturgy that engages and requires catechesis along the way. In other words, catechesis takes place before, during, and after each ritual step.

Significant to the restoration of the RCIA and its vision for catechesis is that it recognizes the historical relationship between liturgy and catechesis. In the early centuries of the Church, liturgy and catechesis were intimately connected and associated with the catechumenate. This was evident through liturgical preaching, which was the main form of catechesis. Liturgy and catechesis were two sides of the same coin. With its restoration, the RCIA reunites both liturgy and catechesis into an integral relationship. I will explore this relationship in more detail later in this book in the discussion on team formation.

The Second Vatican Council and the RCIA

As stated above, the *Rite of Christian Initiation of Adults* is a restored rite of the Church. Interest in renewing the initiation process began in the twentieth century with the early liturgical and catechetical movements—a time where we saw recovery of ancient texts—for example, the *Didache* (Teaching of the Twelve Apostles), an early handbook for liturgy and catechesis.[5] Eventually these early influences led to the mandate of the Second

4. USCCB, *National Catechetical Directory* (Washington, DC: United States Conference of Catholic Bishops, 2005), 10. Note: this document is the only USCCB document that uses page numbers in its citation as opposed to paragraph numbers.

5. Turner, *The Hallelujah Highway*, 14.

Vatican Council to restore the catechumenate. We find explicit evidence of this in *Sacrosanctum concilium* (SC), which states:

> The catechumenate for adults, comprising several distinct stages, is to be restored and brought into use at the discretion of the local ordinary. By this means the time of the catechumenate, which is intended as a period of suitable formation, may be sanctified by sacred rites to be celebrated at successive intervals of time. (64)[6]

In addition, *Christus Dominus* (CD) states:

> Bishops should be especially concerned about catechetical instruction. . . . It should be very carefully imparted, not only to children and adolescents but also to young people and even to adults. . . . They should take steps to reestablish or to improve the adult catechumenate. (14)

Finally, and very significantly, *Ad gentes* (AG) states:

> Those who have received from God the gift of faith in Christ, through the church, should be admitted with liturgical rites to the catechumenate which is not a mere exposition of dogmatic truths and norms of morality, but a period of formation in the entire of christian [*sic*] life, an apprenticeship of suitable duration, during which the disciples will be joined to Christ their teacher. (14)

Without going into too much detail, allow me to offer some brief comments that help situate the *Rite of Christian Initiation of Adults* in the context of the wider vision of the Church. The study and meaning of the Church was a vital question and key theme of the council. *Lumen gentium* (LG), for example, provides the meaning of the nature and mission of the Church, which brought about renewed awareness of *Church* as the People of God. The Church is declared a historical living reality of the saving event of Jesus Christ, and we are a new people living this out in the present time. The emphasis is on Church as a people who believe that Jesus Christ is the Son of God, and we express this belief in our life and in our worship. Moreover, as Church, the baptized have a responsibility to carry on the mission of the Church. This holds great significance to those engaged in initiation ministry.

---

6. References to the documents of the Second Vatican are from Austin Flannery, OP, ed., *Vatican Council II: The Basic Sixteen Documents; Constitutions, Decrees, Declarations* (Collegeville, MN: Liturgical Press, 2014).

Lumen gentium is clear that through our baptism we become a part of the Body of Christ (LG, 7) and through confirmation we are bound more fully to the Church; we "are endowed with the special strength of the holy Spirit" (LG, 11). From the moment of our baptism, we become part of a living community—we cease to live in isolation. All members are formed in the likeness of Jesus Christ, who is the pattern for life (LG, 11). Chapter 2 of *Lumen gentium*, "The People of God," gives powerful statements about who we are as the baptized. This gives momentum to the fact that in the celebration of the Eucharist, where the paschal mystery is made present for us now, we come and remember our baptism, actualizing what it means to be the Body of Christ.

Consequently, with the Second Vatican Council, we experienced a reshaping of pastoral practice that is based on a renewed ecclesiology; this is what grounds the *Rite of Christian Initiation of Adults*. In other words, when seen from a historical perspective, which the Second Vatican Council does, the initiation rites of the Church also affect our view of the meaning and celebration of sacraments in general. This renewed ecclesiology influences the role of the worshiping community in the preparation and in the celebration of the sacraments of initiation.

It is also interesting to realize how initiation ministry came into being in the contemporary Church. After the Second Vatican Council, the *Rite of Christian Initiation of Adults*, also appropriately referred to as the catechumenate, was reborn under the direction of Fr. Balthasar Fisher. From 1964 to 1970 he directed the working group for the reform of the initiation rites. After wrestling with ancient rites, the group came to a consensus that the catechumenate "is a timeless pattern that has both time-bound and timeless elements."[7] Fisher educated the group on the history of the catechumenate, the liturgy, the relevance of the *Apostolic Tradition*, the commitment to pastoral activity, how the catechumenate flourished in the early Church, and its success in missionary lands. The work of this group produced a provisional text in 1966, there was approval from Rome to experiment with it until 1969, and Pope Paul VI approved the text in 1972. In 1974, a provisional English translation was produced;

7. Robert L. Tuzik, *How Firm a Foundation: Leaders of the Liturgical Movement* (Chicago: Liturgy Training Publications, 1990), 131.

in 1986, we had the White Book[8] and, finally, the ritual text was mandated for use in the United States in 1988.

With the vision of the rite in view, in the next chapter I will explore the practice of ministry, which provides the backdrop to forming an effective initiation team.

8. The White Book refers to Rome's confirmation and recognition (*recognitio*) of an English translation of a ritual text, which then becomes an official English translation.

CHAPTER TWO

The Practice of Ministry

In the introduction to the *Rite of Christian Initiation of Adults,* you will find a section titled "Ministries and Offices" (RCIA, 9–16). Throughout these paragraphs, we see various roles for initiation ministry—for example, the community, the sponsor, the godparent, the bishop, priests, deacons, and catechists. Nowhere does the rite mention an initiation team or a coordinator. Experience has shown, however, that in order for initiation ministry to be effective, a collaborative initiation team, under the direction of a knowledgeable coordinator, is essential.

In the previous chapter, I made the point that the Second Vatican Council put into motion a shift in our understanding of ecclesiology, that is, what it means to be the Church. This chapter will expand on this point and explore the impact of the council for the practice of ministry. An appreciation for the practice of ministry that involves the ordained and the nonordained leads to successful and full implementation of the *Rite of Christian Initiation of Adults.* With this in mind, the intention of this chapter is to look at the practice of ministry, which is the background for good and effective team development and formation. First, I will look at the rationale for ministry found in Sacred Scripture and Church documents. Next, I will look at what motivates the practice of ministry. I will focus on the meaning of discipleship, vocation, and discernment and their relationship to ministry. Discipleship, vocation, and discernment are key aspects for living out the gift of baptism and, in turn, one's response to the call to ministry.

In addition to men being called to the priesthood or the permanent diaconate, many laywomen and laymen are called to serve the Church either professionally as lay ecclesial ministers or as dedicated volunteers. Mindful of this important reality, this book promotes an approach to ministry that puts the ordained in pastoral relationship with lay ministers who are called to serve the Church. This is worth our consideration because an initiation team includes both the ordained and nonordained, which is envisioned by the rite. Edward Hahnenberg expresses this relationship extremely well in *Ministries: A Relational Approach*. He writes:

> The baptized have taken up their call to actively serve the reign of God. . . . The ordained priest has been gradually moving into a new, more challenging position: from standing at the apex of a pyramid that was the parish to serving at the center of an active community, from being the minister to becoming a ministerial leader and coordinator of many ministries.[1]

This realization is particularly helpful for the formation of an initiation team.

The practice of ministry involves the pastoral care of people. Concerning the *Rite of Christian Initiation of Adults*, care is given to, in many cases, the stranger—the stranger who comes inquiring about how faith is lived out in and through the Roman Catholic Church. As stated previously, this is a sacred trust. Moreover, "theologically sound ministry is guided by the principle of respect for human dignity. Ministry that is shaped by this theologically informed principle will be compassionate, sensitive, understanding, participatory, and representative of God's ministry."[2] Wow! This is profound and we should not expect anything less from an initiation team.

A Rationale for Ministry: Sacred Scripture

The principles and the vision for the practice of ministry can be found within Sacred Scripture, particularly the New Testament. The Pauline letters are probably the best example of this. Paul was deeply committed to the mission of the Church, and all of his writing is rooted in a deep response to the Good News of Christ. Paul integrated theology and practice in a profound way. He demonstrated heartfelt pastoral concern for the communities to whom he wrote. Moreover, Paul's ministry was centered on three things: proclaiming the Gospel, establishing congregations,

1. Edward P. Hahnenberg, *Ministries: A Relational Approach* (New York: The Crossroads Publishing Company, 2003), 1.

2. Earl E. Shelp and Ronald Sunderland, eds., *A Biblical Basis for Ministry* (Philadelphia: The Westminster Press, 1982), 13.

and nurturing these new congregations.[3] We can see functions associated with preaching, healing, discerning, and teaching with the intent to build up the community. Paul also speaks about many gifts and different forms of service. For example, in 1 Corinthians 12:8–11 he says:

> To one is given through the Spirit the expression of wisdom; to another the expression of knowledge according to the same Spirit; to another faith by the same Spirit; to another gifts of healing by the one Spirit; to another mighty deeds; to another prophecy; to another discernment of spirits; to another variety of tongues; to another interpretation of tongues. But one and the same Spirit produces all of these; distributing them individually to each person as he wishes.

Similarly, in 1 Corinthians 12:28 Paul writes, "Some people God has designated in the church to be, first apostles; second, prophets; third, teachers; then, mighty deeds; then gifts of healing, assistance, [and] administration." Writing to the Ephesians Paul affirms, "And he gave some as apostles, others as prophets, others as evangelists, others as pastors and teachers" (Ephesians 4:11). Finally, in 1 Corinthians 12:4–7, he says, "There are different kinds of spiritual gifts but the same Spirit; there are different forms of service but the same Lord; there are different workings but the same God who produces all of them in everyone. To each individual the manifestation of the Spirit is given for some benefit."

Paul also refers to charisms. This comes from the Greek *charis*, which means grace. Grace is the profound gift of God's loving presence with us. What Paul is trying to emphasize is that God gives us the gifts of faith, hope, and charity. These gifts of our baptism enable us to respond to the call into relationship with Christ and his Body, the Church. These gifts are the essence of discipleship.[4] The appreciation for what it means to live as a disciple, as we will see, leads to our response to the call to ministry. Charisms are particular gifts or talents that are unique to each person. In preparing people for ministry, it is vital that we help them prayerfully discern their gifts for service.

---

3. Victor Paul Furnish, "Theology and Ministry in the Pauline Letters," in Shelp and Sunderland, *A Biblical Basis for Ministry*, 101–144.

4. Kathleen A. Cahalan, *Introducing the Practice of Ministry* (Collegeville, MN: Liturgical Press, 2010), 31.

In the Gospel of John, we find the most profound reference to ministry in the Last Supper discourse. Jesus gives us a vivid picture of what we are called to do: "he rose from supper and took off his outer garments. He took a towel and tied it around his waist. Then he poured water into a basin and began to wash the disciples' feet" (John 13:4–5). This action, a prelude to Jesus' passion, death, and resurrection, demonstrates radical faith, hope, and love. This is a commandment (*mandatum*) to serve one another with love.

Church Documents: The Call to Holiness

I love to read and study documents. For many, Church documents may not be exciting. Even Pope Francis says, "I am aware that nowadays documents do not arouse the same interest as in the past and that they are quickly forgotten" (EG, 25).

In the previous chapter, I mentioned that *Lumen gentium* emphasizes the Church as the People of God. Significantly, LG also dedicates chapter 5 to the "universal call to holiness." This call to holiness is the foundation for all ministry. In my pastoral experience, I have found that many laypeople are both surprised and gratified by what *Lumen gentium* says:

> It is therefore quite clear that all Christians in whatever state or walk of life are called to the fullness of Christian life and to the perfection of charity, and this holiness is conducive to a more human way of living in society here on earth. (40)

The universal call to holiness extends to all! And as more and more men and women recognize this truth, they respond to the call to ministry. Significant to lay ministers, the reality of the universal call to holiness is repeated and affirmed in *Co-Workers in the Vineyard of the Lord: A Resource for Guiding the Development of Lay Ecclesial Ministry.*[5]

Fittingly, Pope Francis gives a new approach to the universal call to holiness in his apostolic exhortation *Gaudete et exsultate* (GE). He states, "My modest goal is to re-pose the call to holiness in a practical way for our own time, with all its risks, challenges and opportunities. For the Lord has chosen each one of us 'to be holy and blameless before him in

5. USCCB, *Co-Workers in the Vineyard of the Lord: A Resource for Guiding the Development of Lay Ecclesial Ministry* (Washington, DC: United States Conference of Catholic Bishops, 2005), 7–8.

love' (Eph 1:4)" (GE, 2).[6] The call to holiness, ours, by virtue of our baptism, is deepened and put into practice as we become aware of the potential held within the lived reality of discipleship, vocation, and discernment.

Discipleship

The *Catechism of the Catholic Church* explains discipleship in this way:

> From the beginning, Jesus associated his disciples with his own life, revealed the mystery of the Kingdom to the disciples and gave them a share in his mission, his joy, and his sufferings[7]. . . . And he proclaimed a mysterious and real communion between his own body and ours: "He who eats my flesh and drinks my blood abides in me, and I in him."[8] (CCC, 787)[9]

It is the gift of baptism that marks us with this call to live as disciples of Jesus Christ. Through baptism, as disciples, we are part of Christ's Body, the Church. The revitalization of the term "Body of Christ" is important and very relevant to initiation ministry. It means that we are members of a body and every member plays a part. Because we are baptized into this Body, as disciples, we have the responsibility to carry out the mission of the Church. In this regard, in his apostolic exhortation *Evangelii gaudium*, Pope Francis reminds us of the responsibility of being a disciple. He writes:

> In virtue of their baptism, all members of the People of God have become missionary disciples (cf. Mt 28:19). All the baptized, whatever their position in the Church or their level of instruction in faith, are agents of evangelization, and it would be insufficient to envisage a plan of evangelization to be carried out by professionals while the rest of the faithful would simply be passive recipients. The new evangelization calls for personal involvement on the part of each of the baptized. (EG, 120)

Today, as the Church needs to experience a profound missionary renewal, there is a kind of preaching that falls to each of us as a daily

6. Pope Francis, *Gaudete et Exsultate: On the Call to Holiness in Today's World* (Huntington, IN: Our Sunday Visitor, 2018).

7. Cf. Mark 1:16–20; 3:13–19; Matthew 13:10–17; Luke 10:17–20; 22:28–30.

8. John 6:56

9. *Catechism of the Catholic Church* (Washington, DC: United States Conference of Catholic Bishops, 1997).

responsibility. It has to do with bringing the Gospel to the people we meet, whether it be our neighbors or complete strangers. "Being a disciple means being constantly ready to bring the love of Jesus to others, and this can happen unexpectedly and in any place on the street, in a city square, during work, on a journey" (EG, 127).

There are many dimensions to what Pope Francis refers to as the "joy of discipleship."[10] A disciple's life is a journey of faith lived in joy: this joy that comes from our attentiveness to the Word of God, which guides our journey and leads to hope in all circumstances. Pope Francis implores us:

> Dear friends, be glad! Do not be afraid of being joyful! Don't be afraid of joy—that joy the Lord gives us when we allow him to enter our lives. Let us allow him to enter our lives and invite us to go out to the margins of life and proclaim the Gospel. Don't be afraid of joy. Have joy and courage![11]

While discipleship is joyful, it also comes with responsibility. Jesus is very clear when it comes to the conditions of discipleship. He lovingly teaches us, "If anyone wishes to come after me, he must deny himself and take up his cross daily and follow me. For whoever wishes to save his life will lose it, but whoever loses his life for my sake will save it" (Luke 9:23–24). There is no getting around it: discipleship means taking up the cross. Sharing in divine life also means going to the cross—to suffer with Christ; it is the cross that leads to redemption. Sharing in the cross of Christ is actually a perfect sign of God's love for us.

This is especially significant for initiation ministers to grasp since the very first ritual step of the rite, the Rite of Acceptance into the Order of Catechumens, marks the new catechumen with the sign of the cross:

> Come forward now with your sponsors to receive the sign of your new way of life as catechumens.
>
> Receive the cross on your forehead. / It is Christ himself who now strengthens you with the sign of his love. / Learn to know and follow him. (RCIA, 55A)

10. See Pope Francis, *The Joy of Discipleship* (Chicago: Loyola Press, 2016).

11. *The Joy of Discipleship*, 35.

If the mark of a catechumen is the cross, then the initiation team must also bear this mark.

We can also learn about discipleship from Mary, the Mother of God. Pope Francis gives beautiful insight to this profound reality. He writes, "As Jesus' first and perfect disciple, Mary lived perpetually immersed in the mystery of God-made-man by contemplating all things in her heart in light of the Holy Spirit, in order to understand and live the will of God."[12] Jesus entrusted Mary to us; "Behold, your mother" (John 19:27). Therefore, as disciples, we are also called to be open to God's presence in our everyday lives and put our firm trust in him. Mary had a unique personal holiness and her intense personal prayer sustained her to follow her son. And at the cross she is the "Mother of Hope."[13] Therefore, as we submit to the cross, Mary is there to bring us to this same hope in order that we remain free from despair.[14]

It is worth mentioning that Avery Cardinal Dulles also took discipleship seriously. Originally, Dulles proposed five approaches or models to explore the theology of the Church in the years following the Second Vatican Council: institution, mystical communion, sacrament, herald, and servant. In his expanded edition of *Models of the Church*, however, he adds a sixth model, "The Church: Community of Disciples."[15] He does this in an effort to highlight the "qualifications for pastoral leadership" and that discipleship is directly related to the model of mystical communion. In addition, he states that "the concept of discipleship also builds bridges to the other four models."[16] He traces the roots of the discipleship model to the New Testament and to Jesus' ministry.[17] Each of the Gospel writers give a specific nuance to the term discipleship, and all of the Gospel writers maintain that disciples practiced love and care for those in need. Disciples were so committed to a particular way of life, a life that centered on Jesus Christ. As you can see, discipleship is clearly about identity, an

---

12. *The Joy of Discipleship*, 84.

13. Raniero Cantalamessa, *Mary: Mirror of the Church*, trans. Frances Lonergan Villa (Collegeville, MN: Liturgical Press, 1992), 110.

14. Cantalamessa, *Mary*, 114.

15. See Avery Cardinal Dulles, *Models of the Church* (New York: Image Books/Doubleday, 2002), chapter 13.

16. Dulles, *Models of the Church*, 197.

17. Dulles, *Models of the Church*, 198.

identity that puts us in relationship with the Trinity. Sadly, this often goes unrecognized.

Recognizing and cherishing discipleship is key to fruitful initiation ministry. Initiation ministers, as well as the entire parish, show inquirers, catechumens, candidates, the elect, and neophytes how to become "intentional disciples"[18] through witness to a way of life lived out in and through the Roman Catholic Church. In *Disciples Making Disciples: The Role of the Assembly in Christian Initiation*, Victoria Tufano invites us to remember, "Christianity is not simply a set of beliefs to which we give intellectual agreement. It is a way of life based on a relationship with God, who has revealed himself and what he desires of us and for us through Jesus Christ. Part of being a Christian is witnessing to our faith."[19]

In a very real way, discipleship puts our lives on a path toward an encounter with Christ and reveals for us the rich possibilities that come with the Christian story. Initiation ministers give witness to this story, and this is not only the sign of a true disciple but also central to evangelization. It is helpful to consider what the United States bishops offer for initiation ministry in *Go and Make Disciples: A National Plan and Strategy for Catholic Evangelization in the United States*. They write:

> We present to you, our Catholic sisters and brothers, this plan and strategy of evangelization because the fire of Jesus burns even today. We, your brothers and your bishops, profess our faith in Christ Jesus, in the revelation that he is in the kingdom that he proclaimed, and in the Church that he founded. We proclaim that, through our faith, the stories of Christ continue and that our lives are part of the story of salvation. (4)[20]

Vocation

"Vocation" comes from the Latin *vocare*, meaning to call. The call of all the baptized is to discipleship. And the call to ministry flows from this. As a married woman, I have always felt called to serve the Church and

---

18. See Sherry Weddell, *Forming Intentional Disciples* (Huntington, IN: Our Sunday Visitor, 2012).

19. Victoria M. Tufano, *Disciples Making Disciples: The Role of the Assembly in Christian Initiation* (Chicago: Liturgy Training Publications, 2017).

20. USCCB, *Go and Make Disciples,* 10th ann. English and Spanish ed. (Washington, DC: United States Conference of Catholic Bishops, 2002).

have had the honor of serving in various ministries for over thirty years. I consider my vocation to ministry to be a vocation within a vocation. For some people, however, the word *vocation* is still limited to being called to the priesthood or a religious community. This is often reflected in prayers of the faithful and bulletin articles. Following the Second Vatican Council, however, the Church began to understand vocation in a broader, more inclusive sense. Vocation, in its broadest understanding, reflects a more biblical and traditional vision of God's presence in the world.[21] It means that God calls everyone in a variety of ways, and this includes the call to ministry.

This understanding of vocation is reflected in *Lumen gentium*, which, as we saw above, verifies the universal call to holiness.[22] In addition, the *Catechism of the Catholic Church* affirms this call to holiness in regard to the vocation of lay ministers. The CCC says:

> The laity can also feel called, or in fact be called, to cooperate with their pastors in the service of the ecclesial community, for the sake of its growth and life. This can be done through the exercise of different kinds of ministries according to the grace and charisms which the Lord has been pleased to bestow on them.[23] (CCC, 910)

Definitively, in this same regard, Thomas O'Meara says, "Ministry has moved from being a vocation for a few to being a gift and work of many, a facet of baptized life."[24]

The reality is we are baptized into a community that is ministerial; we are commissioned to serve. Jesus invited his followers into a life of service, not passivity. The call or vocation to ministry originates in baptism. And, as the baptized, we need to take the time to ponder and discern how we are called to serve the parish community that we have been incorporated into through the grace-filled action of the Trinity in baptism.

---

21. See Edward P. Hahnenberg, *Awakening Vocation: A Theology of Christian Call* (Collegeville, MN: Liturgical Press, 2010).

22. See chapter 5 of *Lumen gentium*.

23. Paul VI, *Evangelii nuntiandi*, 73.

24. Thomas F. O'Meara, OP, *Theology of Ministry* (New York: Paulist Press, 1999), 5.

Discernment

In my experience, prayer and reflection are valuable parts of team meetings. The prayer and reflection a team shares teaches the group to prayerfully "sift through"[25] our experiences, feelings, and emotions. These words lead us toward a way of life that ultimately brings us to peace and holiness.

It is important to realize that discernment is at the heart of our identity as disciples. Donna Steffen provides rich insight about this important task. She writes:

> Discipleship involves living with and in the being of Christ. . . . We know the heart of this person who believed until death and beyond in the Holy One, the God who is faithful and full of limitless love. We know this Jesus who was so deeply connected with God, even in his human nature, that he always lived out of this relationship. . . . We clearly see Jesus listening to the Spirit, discerning God's way, in the scene of the temptations in the desert (Matthew 4:1–11). Jesus discerns.[26]

So as faithful disciples we must also discern. In doing so, we imitate the master and ultimately become the master. Only then, with complete trust, can we listen for the surprising graces of a Spirit-filled life.

Every period and ritual step in the *Rite of Christian Initiation of Adults* calls for discernment on the part of the participants. Therefore, initiation ministers need to understand the discernment process in their own life. Prayerful discernment helps us to navigate through the obstacles by taking the time to find out what God is calling us to in a particular moment. Therefore, as disciples who serve the Church through initiation ministry, give priority to the art of discernment. Only then can we help others recognize God's action and presence in their lives as they journey through the initiation process.

---

25. Donna Steffens, SC, *Discernment in Christian Initiation* (Chicago: Liturgy Training Publications, 2018), 6.

26. Steffens, *Discernment in Christian Initiation*, 1.

Guided by Virtues

The *Catechism of the Catholic Church* says:

> A virtue is an habitual and firm disposition to do the good. It allows the person not only to perform good acts, but to give the best of himself. The virtuous person tends toward the good with all his sensory and spiritual power; he pursues the good and chooses it in concrete actions. (CCC, 1803)

Once we understand this, we realize that at a basic level, the call to holiness also involves an awareness of the responsibilities and moral demands that come with being a disciple, and especially with the call to the practice of ministry. Those engaged in ministry need to act in ways that are responsive to the action and presence of God in their lives.[27] All of the dimensions of formation should lead us to make virtue an integral part of who we are and the mission we serve. In other words, the practice of ministry calls us to be people of integrity—truthful, reliable, loyal, and honest. In this way, we will always protect the dignity of those whom we serve and those with whom we serve.

Ministerial Relationships, Rooted in the Sacraments of Initiation

Co-Workers in the Vineyard of the Lord: A Resource for Guiding the Development of Lay Ecclesial Ministry is a pastoral guide affirming the many lay ministers serving in various ministerial roles. The document offers theological foundations, discernment, and suitability for ministry, formation, authorization, and policies and practices for the ministerial workplace. One distinguishing aspect, which is related to initiation ministry, can be found in the section "Ministry: Serving the Church and Its Mission," which acknowledges that all the faithful have a share in the Church's mission. In recognition of different gifts for different roles, it states:

> Ministerial relationships are grounded first in what all members of Christ's Body have in common. Through their sacramental initiation all are established in a personal relationship with Christ and in a network of relationships with the communion of the People of God. The per-

27. See Richard M. Gula, SS, *Ethics in Pastoral Ministry* (Mahwah, NJ: Paulist Press, 1996).

> sonal discipleship of each individual makes possible a community of disciples formed by and for the mission of Christ.[28]

All members of the Body of Christ have sacramental initiation in common. Baptism, confirmation, and Eucharist impact who we are as Christians and, therefore, have a profound effect on who we are as initiation ministers. There is no doubt the *Rite of Christian Initiation of Adults* has revitalized the meaning of Christian initiation for the entire parish community. At every Easter Vigil, it is not uncommon for those baptized as infants to recognize the depth of meaning hidden within the ritual action of their own baptism celebrated years ago. This deepened awareness opens us up to great possibilities for living the Christin life. The call to ministry is born in and through the waters of baptism. Remember, Jesus' public ministry began after he was baptized. In this same regard, *Co-Workers in the Vineyard of the Lord* also reminds us that "by their baptismal incorporation into the Body of Christ, lay persons are also equipped with gifts and graces to build up the Church from within, in cooperation with the hierarchy and under its direction."[29]

Baptism is the foundation for discipleship, vocation, and discernment. It is the impetus for the universal call to holiness and the acknowledgment of charisms for ministry. Confirmation strengthens our identity as disciples, and the Eucharist, the only repeatable sacrament of initiation, nourishes us with Christ's own Body and Blood so that we may serve others with the conviction and courage of true witnesses to the life, death, and resurrection of Jesus Christ.[30]

This chapter serves as the inspiration to engage men and women in the practice of ministry. At its best, an initiation team consists of ordained and nonordained persons working in relationship to ensure full implementation of the RCIA. In a way, the initiation team is the face

---

28. USCCB, *Co-Workers in the Vineyard of the Lord: A Resource for Guiding the Development of Lay Ecclesial Ministry* (Washington, DC: United States Conference of Catholic Bishops, 2005), 21.

29. *Co-Workers*, 12. See CL, nos. 23–24; also see AA, no. 24, for distinctions in regard to the need for lay activity to be recognized by the hierarchy.

30. Also see Donna Eschenauer, "The Sacraments of Initiation: A Guiding Theme for the Future of Lay Ecclesial Ministry," in *Reflections on Renewal Lay Ecclesial Ministry and the Church*, ed. Donna M. Eschenauer and Harold Daly Horell (Collegeville, MN: Liturgical Press, 2011), 114–124.

of the parish. Therefore, inquirers, catechumens, candidates, the elect, and neophytes need to see in the team what it means to be a disciple.

Having set the stage for the practice of ministry, in the next chapter, I will emphasize the classical dimensions of formation for those called to the service of the Church. Lay ministers, as well as the ordained, deserve a high standard of holistic formation. The four areas of formation —human, spiritual, pastoral, and intellectual—familiar to priesthood and the permanent diaconate also lay the foundation for the formation of lay ministers.[31]

31. *Co-Workers*, 34.

CHAPTER THREE

Dimensions of Formation for Ministry

In the last chapter, we looked at the practice of ministry as being rooted in baptism and the universal call to holiness. We also looked at the meaning of discipleship—discipleship that takes the call to participate in the ministry of the Church as well as a way of life grounded in discernment seriously. This is a lifelong process of development that involves initial and ongoing formation. The four classic dimensions of formation for both ordained and nonordained ministers are human, spiritual, pastoral, and intellectual.[1]

Proper attention and integration of the four dimensions of formation lead to the fruitful practice of ministry. For our purposes, I will refer to *Co-Workers in the Vineyard of the Lord,* which provides explanation and methods for formation in all four areas.[2]

Human Formation

> *Human formation seeks to develop the lay ecclesial minister's human qualities and character, fostering a healthy and well-balanced personality, for the sake of both personal growth and ministerial service.*[3]

The call to ministry begins with the human vocation. In other words, those engaged in ministry need to develop a basic understanding of themselves and demonstrate a healthy lifestyle that is indicative of

1. All four dimensions of formation are found in the USCCB's *Program of Priestly Formation,* 5th ed. (68–257), the USCCB's *National Directory for the Formation, Ministry, and Life of the Permanent Deacons in the United States* (104–133), and *Co-Workers in the Vineyard of the Lord: A Resource for Guiding the Development of Lay Ecclesial Ministry* (p. 33–49). Significantly, the four areas of formation are consistent for clergy and laity; this complies with the *Code of Canon Law,* which requires proper preparation for all ministry (CIC, 235, 236, 237).

2. See *Co-Workers,* 33–53.

3. *Co-Workers,* 36.

good self-care. They must understand the value of responsibility, compassion, integrity, interpersonal boundaries, and confidentiality. In relationship to ministerial choices a person must be able to understand their abilities and gifts—their charisms—as well as what they lack so that they might learn the art of collaboration. An understanding of family systems[4] in relationship to the Church's teaching on family life and an appreciation for cultural diversity is also key to good ministerial practice.

Human formation is undoubtedly a lifelong process; however, human development is fostered, for example, through spiritual direction, small faith-sharing communities, pastoral supervision, and theological reflection.

Spiritual Formation

> *Spiritual formation aims to arouse and animate true hunger for holiness, desire for union with the Father through Christ in the Spirit, daily growing in love of God and neighbor in life and ministry, and the practices of prayer and spirituality that foster these attitudes and dispositions. It promotes and strengthens that fundamental conversion that places God, and not oneself, at the center of one's life. Openness to ongoing conversion is a prerequisite for fruitful spiritual formation.*[5]

Formation in the spiritual life aids in the development of one's desire to live their faith fully. It is an ongoing desire to recognize God's action and presence in the everyday circumstances of life, even the most ordinary. As noted in the previous chapter, through baptism we are intimately united to God, through Christ, in the power of the Holy Spirit. The spiritual life is an invitation to grow in this relationship. It is an invitation to know God and to know oneself at a deeper level. This may entail a deepened awareness of sin, which is an invitation to ongoing conversion. Another way to understand the spiritual life it is to explore

4. For more on family systems, see National Conference of Catholic Bishops, *A Family Perspective in Church and Society* (1998), chapter 4; for more on family life, see John Paul II, *The Role of the Christian Family in the Modern World* (*Familiaris consortio*) (1982), part 3; Pope Francis, *The Joy of Love On Love and the Family* (*Amoris laetitia*) (2016).

5. *Co-Workers*, 38.

the lives of the saints. They can teach us what it means to encounter Christ and to understand, at a deeper level, what it means to do God's will, which is key to the spiritual life.

Fruitful ministry is grounded in a personal encounter with Jesus Christ. And this encounter is nourished by reading and reflecting on the Word of God, as well as by participating in the celebration of liturgy and the sacraments, particularly the Eucharist. Most significant, living the spiritual life means embracing the paschal mystery, which means making the passion, death, and resurrection of Jesus Christ the pattern for living.

Spiritual formation for ministry helps us to discover different forms of prayer and devotion. In addition, a spiritual director can help with discernment and direct us on how to navigate the sometimes hard to define road to holiness. Again, theological reflection is a skill to be pursued because it helps us to consider where God is in a particular situation. Patricia O'Connell Killen and John DeBeer state it most clearly:

> Theological reflection is the discipline of exploring individual and corporate experience in conversation with the wisdom of a religious heritage. The conversation is a genuine dialogue that seeks to hear from our own beliefs, actions, and perspectives, as well as those of the tradition. It respects the integrity of both. Theological reflection therefore may confirm, challenge, clarify, and expand how we understand our own experience and how we understand the religious tradition. The outcome is truth and meaning for living.[6]

It is evident that theological reflection is closely related to discernment, which I discussed in the last chapter. It is a process for seeking meaning and making choices that reflect a Catholic Christian way of life that is grounded in the Gospel. It helps us integrate our ordinary, everyday life experience with our faith.

The goal of the spiritual life is union with God. It is prayerful listening to know God's desire for us. The spiritual life strengthens our identity as disciples. And Jesus shares the privilege of discipleship with us. In the proclamation of the Gospel according to Luke, we hear, "Turning to the disciples in private he said, 'Blessed are the eyes that see

---

6. Patricia O'Connell Killen and John DeBeer, *The Art of Theological Reflection* (New York: The Crossroad Publishing Company, 1994), viii.

what you see. For I say to you, many prophets and kings desire to see what you see, but did not see it, and to hear what you hear, but did not hear it'" (Luke 10:23-24).

Intellectual Formation

> *Intellectual formation seeks to develop the lay ecclesial minister's understanding and appreciation of the Catholic faith, which is rooted in God's revelation and embodied in the living tradition of the Church. It consists chiefly of study of the sacred sciences but draws also upon a wide range of other disciplines: philosophy, literature and the arts, psychology, sociology, counseling, medical ethics, culture and language studies, business administration, leadership and organizational development, law, and so on.*[7]

For the practice of ministry, it is increasingly important to have appropriate intellectual formation in Catholic Church teaching. It is important to realize that this formation actually strengthens and nourishes the human, the spiritual, and the pastoral dimensions of formation. In this regard, *Co-Workers in the Vineyard of the Lord* aptly points out, "Thus, their faith, spirituality, and pastoral practice can be strengthened, and they will become theologically well-formed pastoral ministers: knowing the breadth of Church teaching and the richly varied theological tradition, and able to access and use these resources to meet the needs of ministry today."[8]

Intellectual formation is the study of theology that advances the work of catechesis. It includes the study of Sacred Scripture and dogmatic theology, which includes the study of the Trinity, Christ, and the Church; it includes Church history, liturgy and sacraments, moral theology, Catholic social teaching, spirituality, pastoral theology, and canon law.

The aspect of intellectual formation should not be overwhelming to anyone who is called to ministry. In addition to studying the RCIA ritual text, coordinators can collaborate with other pastoral staff members

7. *Co-Workers*, 42–43.

8. *Co-Workers*, 44.

or link with diocesan programs to find resourceful ways to offer adult faith formation. For example, an exploration on the *Catechism of the Catholic Church* and basic classes in Scripture, spirituality, and liturgy would be beneficial to volunteer ministers. This dimension of formation should be conducive to adult learning and include various methods that will engage participants for a more effective learning experience. Methods can include, for example, lecture, discussion, independent study, and distance learning.[9]

Pastoral Formation

> *Pastoral formation cultivates the knowledge, attitudes, and skills that directly pertain to effective functioning in the ministry setting and that also pertain to pastoral administration that supports direct ministry.*[10]

Pastoral formation links the human, spiritual, and intellectual dimensions of formation with the practice of ministry. Its goal is to lead a person to successful and effective performance in a ministerial setting. Elements of pastoral formation include leading prayer, facilitating group discussion, skills for evangelization and catechesis, sensitivity to family life, development of communication and listening skills, collaboration skills, awareness of the contemporary world, conflict management skills, organizational skills, and understanding the discernment of gifts. These skills are essential for initiation ministers and should be included in their formation.

The practice of ministry in your parish will be successful when the four dimensions of formation are well integrated into ministry formation. Successful parish or diocesan programs envision ministry formation as a holistic process that keeps these four areas of formation in sight. Ministry training of this sort is important for the professional minister as well as for volunteers. This ideal serves the parish, the Church, the minister, and all who participate in and all who seek to participate in the life of the parish.

---

9. See USCCB, *Our Hearts Were Burning within Us: A Pastoral Plan for Adult Faith Formation in the United States* (Washington, DC: United States Conference of Catholic Bishops, 1999).

10. *Co-Workers*, 47.

Keep in mind that formation for ministry includes initial formation and, most important, ongoing formation, which is also explored in chapter 8, for the duration of service to a particular ministry. This is indispensable for the ordained and nonordained. Both financial and material resources should be allocated for good, solid ongoing formation through workshops, retreat days, conferences, virtual workshops, and hybrid or online resources.

In order to provide comprehensive formation, initiation coordinators could incorporate the four dimensions of formation into team meetings. An even more efficient idea might be to collaborate with the coordinator or director of adult faith formation to explore formation possibilities. For example, human formation may include a guest speaker on the topic of Catholic human sexuality, interpersonal boundaries, personal wellness, family systems, and cultural diversity. Pastoral formation could include topics such as leadership skills for ministry, leading group discussions, listening skills, catechetical methodology, leading prayer, communication skills, collaboration skills for ministry, and organizational skills for ministry. Spiritual formation could include a retreat day, a session on the different forms of prayer and devotion, and praying with scripture using *lectio divina*. Intellectual formation nourishes the human, pastoral, and spiritual aspects of formation and, in addition to exploring a theology of ministry, can, as already mentioned, include an exploration on the *Catechism of the Catholic Church* and basic classes in Scripture, spirituality, and liturgy.

CHAPTER FOUR

The Practice of Initiation Ministry

The following decree from the *Rite of Christian Initiation of Adults*, envisions the full implementation of the rite within the parishes of the dioceses of the United States.

> From 1 September 1988 the use of the *Rite of Christian Initiation of Adults* is mandatory in the dioceses of the United States of America. From that day forward no other English version may be used. (RCIA, Decree)

The decree signals a move beyond a school-year model or a one-on-one model of instruction for inquirers with sacraments taking place in private. Therefore, the practice of initiation ministry takes the following words from the rite to heart:

> This rite includes not simply the celebration of the sacraments of baptism, confirmation, and eucharist, but also all the rites belonging to the catechumenate. Endorsed by the ancient practice of the Church, a catechumenate that would be suited to contemporary missionary activity in all regions was so widely requested that the Second Vatican Council decreed its restoration, revision, and adaptation to local traditions. (RCIA Introduction, 2)

Significantly, the rite also envisions that it be a gradual process that takes place in the midst of the community (RCIA Introduction, 4). As noted in chapter 1, the *Rite of Christian Initiation of Adults* is made up of specific periods, each with their own character and ritual steps that require discernment on the part of the participant.

The vision for Christian initiation expressed in the rite is sheer wisdom and comes naturally to a parish that makes liturgy and the celebration of sacraments the center of parish life. Moreover, a parish that makes liturgy and sacraments its central activity implicitly promotes a deep liturgical spirituality that shapes a way of life. In addition, a parish that perceives liturgy and sacraments in this way can better understand the pivotal paragraph from the *Rite of Christian Initiation of Adults*, Introduction, which states:

> [T]he people of God, as represented by the local Church, should understand and show by their concern that the initiation of adults is the responsibility of all the baptized. Therefore the community must always be fully prepared in the pursuit of its apostolic vocation to give help to those who are searching for Christ. (RCIA Introduction, 9)

This paragraph has considerable ramifications for the practice of initiation ministry and, ultimately, the lived experience of liturgy, which is the fundamental goal of Christian initiation.

Chapters 1 through 3 of this book provided the necessary background for a comprehensive understanding of the practice of ministry. This chapter is more specific to Christian initiation ministry. It discusses initiation ministry by looking at the significance of a liturgical spirituality and the benefit of an awareness of the meaning of the sacraments of initiation.

Liturgical Spirituality

It is no secret that my initial introduction to initiation ministry left a lasting impression on me. After my first experience as a sponsor, I became engaged in living my Catholic faith in a different way. I now recognize that during this time the stirrings of a love for liturgy and a desire to develop an understanding of liturgy through study were born. At a deeper level, however, this experience was a personal response that brought me into the transformative experience of a liturgical spirituality.

A liturgical spirituality invites us to allow the ritual prayer of the Church to shape our way of being in the world. It influences who we are at our core and has an impact on our relationship with God and with all of creation. When a liturgical spirituality takes root in us, our life is directed by the Word of God, and, at the same time, in and through the sacraments we encounter Jesus Christ in a unique and profound way.

In the same way that rituals are important to our everyday life experiences like eating, waking up, going to sleep, and celebrating a birthday or an anniversary, rituals are important for the Church. The Church's rituals make the mystery of God present for us—here and now. Goffredo

Boselli says it most powerfully: "Through liturgy, the mystery is revealed, communicated, made known. This is to say that liturgy is a theological act, an action of God, and for this reason it accomplishes what it signifies."[1]

In the introduction to this book, I quoted Liam G. Walsh who says, "Christians are known as people of words: they have a story to tell about how God has given eternal life to humans and a doctrine about the meaning of the story. And when they gather to celebrate the life they live and the story they tell, they practice rites."[2] While this is true, we are also a people of actions—we worship with our bodies and the things of the earth, for example, bread, wine, oil, candles.[3] Gestures and bodily postures are also important in the celebration of liturgy. Notably, gestures and bodily postures occupy a section in the *General Instruction on the Roman Missal* (GIRM), which states:

> The gestures and bodily postures of both the Priest, the Deacon, and the ministers, and also of the people, must be conducive to making the entire celebration resplendent with beauty and noble simplicity, to making clear the true and full meaning of its different parts, and to fostering the participation of all. (42)[4]

In his commentary on the *General Instruction on the Roman Missal,* Joseph DeGrocco emphasizes, "Insofar as liturgy is enacted theology, gestures and bodily postures are important components of the 'language' of liturgy, components that help to give expression to the mystery in which all are called to participate."[5] Just as the words we proclaim and pray, what we do with our bodies speaks about who we are as the People of God. Initiation ministers should be conscious of how they sit, stand, kneel, and walk in procession. These actions give witness to who we are and how we pray.

Most important, a liturgical spirituality gives us a paschal identity, that is, a life patterned on the paschal mystery—the mystery of the death

1. Goffredo Boselli, *The Spiritual Meaning of the Liturgy: School of Prayer, Source of Life,* trans. Barry Hudock (Collegeville, MN: Liturgical Press, 2014), 4.

2. Liam G. Walsh, OP, *Sacraments of Initiation*, xiii.

3. See Michael Ruzicki, Victoria M. Tufano, D. Todd Williamson, and Terry Navarro, *Signs and Symbols of the Liturgy: An Experience of Ritual and Catechesis* (Chicago: Liturgy Training Publications, 2018), 1.

4. USCCB, *The General Instruction of the Roman Missal* (Washington, DC: United States Conference of Catholic Bishops, 2011).

5. Joseph DeGrocco, *A Pastoral Commentary on the General Instruction on the Roman Missal* (Chicago: Liturgy Training Publications, 2011), 29.

and resurrection of Jesus, the Christ. This journey into the mystery of God is expressed in and through the liturgy, and it forms and shapes us. No less is true for the *Rite of Christian Initiation of Adults*.

The *Rite of Christian Initiation of Adults* restored and renewed the capacity to develop a liturgical spirituality for those entering the Church, initiation ministers, and the entire community of the baptized. In particular, the rite instills a deeper appreciation for sacraments of initiation—baptism, confirmation, and Eucharist. These three sacraments form our identity as Christians. Those involved in initiation ministry need to reflect on the meaning of these sacraments in their own lives, and this begins with understanding and contemplating the rites. In other words, we are called to be engaged in a lifelong process of mystagogy, "a true and proper theology of the liturgical mystery, revealing the mystery of Christ."[6]

The Sacraments of Initiation

Sacraments are privileged points of encounter with God. They are also ecclesial, and therefore they affect not only one's relationship with God but also one's relationship to the People of God. Sacraments remember and celebrate the paschal mystery—they draw their effectivity from Christ's passion, death, and resurrection. Therefore, they bring Christ's redemption to us now.

It is extremely helpful for those involved in initiation ministry to develop a deepened understanding of the sacraments, particularly the sacraments of initiation, for their own life. Remember that, in chapter 2, I made the claim that the call or vocation to ministry comes from our baptism. Therefore, reflection on baptism, as well as confirmation and Eucharist, provides key insight for the practice of initiation ministry.

Significantly, the General Introduction to the RCIA, referring to *Lumen gentium*, paragraph 31, states that "the three sacraments of Christian initiation closely combine to bring us, the faithful of Christ, to his full stature and to enable us to carry out the mission of the entire people of God in the Church and in the world" (RCIA, Christian Initiation General Introduction, 2).

---

6. Boselli, *The Spiritual Meaning of the Liturgy*, 15.

Baptism

The general introduction of the RCIA says that baptism is "the door to life and to the kingdom of God. . . . Baptism is therefore, above all, the sacrament of that faith by which, enlightened by the grace of the Holy Spirit, we respond to the Gospel of Christ" (3). Pertinent to our understanding, it goes on to say that "baptism is the sacrament by which its recipients are incorporated into the Church and are built up together in the Spirit into a house where God lives" (4). Moreover, "Baptism, the cleansing with water by the power of the living word, washes away every stain of sin, original and personal, and makes us into sharers in God's own life" (5). Finally, and very significantly, it says, "Those who are baptized are united to Christ in a death like his; buried with him in death, they are given life again with him, and with him they rise again. For baptism recalls and makes present the paschal mystery itself, because in baptism we pass from the death of sin into life" (6).

The practice of initiation ministry beckons us to live out the truths of this sacrament. It calls us to wake up every day and commit to living out a ritual that lives on in us and is reflected in our way of being in the world. Having a deepened understanding of baptism in our own lives will certainly make the practice of initiation ministry more fruitful.

Confirmation

Because of current pastoral practice, the rich meaning of the sacrament of confirmation is often eclipsed. The *Rite of Christian Initiation of Adults,* however, explicitly claims confirmation as a sacrament of initiation, which is celebrated directly after baptism (RCIA, 231–236). The rite provides the fuller meaning of confirmation stating:

> My dear newly baptized, born again in Christ by baptism, you have become members of Christ and of his priestly people. Now you are to share in the outpouring of the Holy Spirit among us, the Spirit sent by the Lord upon his apostles at Pentecost and given by them and their successors to be baptized.
>
> The promised strength of the Holy Spirit, which you are to receive, will make you more like Christ and help you to be witnesses to his suffering,

> death, and resurrection. It will strengthen you to be active members of the Church and to build up the Body of Christ in faith and love. (RCIA, 233)

It is helpful to note that the newly revised 2016 *Order of Confirmation* (OC) also provides clarity as it repeats the original decree from 1971 that states:

> Through the sacrament of confirmation the Apostles themselves and the Bishops, who are their successors, have handed on to the baptized the special gift of the Holy Spirit, promised by Christ the Lord and poured out upon the Apostles at Pentecost. With its help, initiation in the Christian life is so brought to completion that the faithful, strengthened by heavenly power, go forth as true witnesses of Christ in word and example, and are bound more closely to the Church. (OC, Decree)[7]

The *Apostolic Constitution on the Sacrament of Confirmation*, written by Pope St. Paul VI, provides further meaning to the sacrament of confirmation. One key point relevant to our discussion is as follows:

> [T]he Second Vatican Ecumenical Council devoted special attention to these Sacraments of Initiation, prescribing that the rites be suitably revised. . . . [I]t is now fitting to publish a Rite of Confirmation, so that the unity of Christian Initiation may be shown in its true light.

The understanding of confirmation shifted throughout history.[8] Originally, the anointing after baptism, eventually celebrated as the sacrament of confirmation, became associated with choice, responsibility, and maturity. With the Second Vatican Council's *Sacrosanctum concilium*, however, confirmation's connection with baptism is affirmed. *Sacrosanctum concilium* is clear:

> The rite of Confirmation is to be revised also so that the intimate connection of this sacrament with the whole of the Christian initiation may more clearly appear. For this reason the renewal of baptismal promises should fittingly precede the reception of the sacrament. (SC, 71)

In addition, the effects of this sacrament are clearly noted in *Lumen gentium*:

---

7. *The Order of Confirmation* (Washington, DC: United States Conference of Catholic Bishops, 2016).

8. See Paul Turner, *Ages of Initiation: The First Two Christian Millennia* (Collegeville, MN: Liturgical Press, 2000).

> Incorporated into the Church by baptism, the faithful are appointed by their baptismal character to Christian religious worship. . . . By the sacrament of confirmation they are *more perfectly bound to the Church and are endowed with the special strength of the Holy Spirit. Hence they are true witnesses of Christ.* . . . Taking part in the eucharistic sacrifice, the source and summit of the Christian life, they offer the divine victim to God and themselves with it. (LG, 11; emphasis added)

We see this very clearly in the *Rite of Christian Initiation of Adults*:

> The conjunction of the two celebrations signifies the unity of the paschal mystery, the close link between the mission of the Son and the outpouring of the Holy Spirit, and the connection between the two sacraments through which the Son and the Holy Spirit come with the Father to those who are baptized. (RCIA, 215)

Eucharist

We are all familiar with the phrase from *Lumen gentium* that the Eucharist is the "source and summit of the Christian life" (11). I think, however, the meaning of the phrase warrants more attention, because the fact remains that the celebration of the Eucharist is the most sacred activity of the parish. St. John Paul II was well aware of a deficiency in our thought, and in his last encyclical, *Ecclesia de Eucharistia*, he reinforces Vatican II and emphasizes that "The Church draws her life from the Eucharist" (1).[9] This sacred action enacts what Christ did on the night he was betrayed. He instituted the Eucharist. In other words, he gave of himself in perfect love. *Sacrosanctum concilium* further explains:

> He did this in order to perpetuate the sacrifice of the cross throughout the centuries until he should come again and in this way to entrust to his beloved Bride, the Church, a memorial of his death and resurrection: a sacrament of love, a sign of unity, a bond of charity, a paschal banquet "in which Christ is eaten, the heart is filled with grace, and a pledge of future glory given to us." (SC, 47)

---

9. John Paul II, "*Ecclesia de Eucharistia*: On the Eucharist in Its Relationship to the Church," in *The Liturgy Documents: Volume One* (Chicago: Liturgy Training Publications, 2012), 229–260.

Sadly, Christ's presence in the Eucharist is, in many ways, obscured or not even recognized. The powerful words from *Sacrosanctum concilium* encapsulate the Church's spiritual treasure.

> To accomplish so great a work, Christ is always present in his Church, especially in its liturgical celebrations. He is present in the sacrifice of the Mass, not only in the person of his minister, "the same now offering, through the ministry of priests, who formerly offered himself on the cross," but especially under the eucharistic elements. . . . He is present in his word, since it is he himself who speaks when the holy scriptures are read in the Church. (SC, 7)

From a liturgical standpoint, and for the purpose of initiation ministry, it is important to remember that Vatican II also recovered the Eucharist as a sacrament of initiation. Baptism and confirmation are fulfilled in the celebration of the Eucharist. In this regard, the *Catechism of the Catholic Church* is clear, "The holy Eucharist completes Christian initiation" (1322). The Eucharist, notably, the only repeatable sacrament of initiation, nourishes us for living the Christian life. And it is the *Rite of Christian Initiation of Adults* that helps further this understanding for the entire parish. Not to be missed, in the third step, the Celebration of the Sacraments of Initiation, during the Liturgy of the Eucharist, the rubric says:

> Before saying "This is the Lamb of God," the celebrant may briefly remind the neophytes of the preeminence of the eucharist, which is the climax of their initiation and the center of the whole Christian life. (RCIA, 243)

After so many years of serving in pastoral ministry, I am convinced that the practice of initiation ministry is rooted in a liturgical spirituality and gains its momentum from the sacraments of initiation. The coordinator of Christian initiation needs to be aware of this and move beyond mere administration.[10] They need to develop and form a team that is committed to the mission of this ministry and in that formation reinforce the depth and underlying essence of the liturgy.

---

10. Donna M. Eschenauer, *The Role of the Coordinator in Christian Initiation: A Pastoral and Practical Guide* (Chicago: Liturgy Training Publications, 2017), 64.

Initiation ministry has the potential to greatly affect parish life and serve as a model for all ministry, especially the educational ministry of the Church. The big question is how do we do this? How do we facilitate the grandeur of a liturgical spirituality? It takes people: clergy and laity who are called, gifted, and committed for this work. Based on my own pastoral experience, I am convinced that this approach holds the potential to successfully guide initiation ministry. The coordinator of Christian initiation and the initiation team, in collaboration with the clergy and other ministers, can make all the difference.

With the practice of initiation ministry in sight, the next chapter will provide some guidance in regard to the role of the parish community in relation to the initiation team.

CHAPTER FIVE

The Parish Community and Initiation

In the last chapter, we looked at the practice of initiation ministry. We also looked at initiation ministry as rooted in a liturgical spirituality where the ritual prayer of the Church forms and shapes us as disciples of Jesus Christ. In addition, we looked at the how the sacraments of initiation provide key insight for our Catholic Christian identity and, therefore, highly influence the practice of initiation ministry. This chapter highlights the role of the parish community as the primary minister of initiation and its relation to the initiation team.

In her classic work *Fashion Me a People: Curriculum in the Church*, Maria Harris views curriculum as the course of the Church's life.[1] This inevitably flows from the realization of who we are as the baptized and confirmed—a people called to a particular way of being in the world. The Church is a people on a mission, sent to reveal the action and presence of God in all things, at all times. The Church is a people called to educate, that is, to participate in the work of forming and re-forming; unfolding and discovering; empowering and reappropriating new insights for living more deeply in our time. Curriculum viewed in this way reflects a lifelong, life-wide journey through which the People of God embark on new and exhilarating experiences that continually invite us to enter more deeply into the reality of what it means to be a Catholic Christian in the world today.

I will never forget the impact that newly elected Pope Francis had on me when he invited those gathered at St. Peter's Square on March 13,

Sections of this chapter were adapted from Donna M. Eschenauer, "The People of God and the *Rite of Christian Initiation of Adults*: Forming and Re-forming the Life of the Church," *Catechumenate: A Journal of Christian Initiation* 35, no. 5 (September 2013): 28–37.

1. Maria Harris, *Fashion Me a People: Curriculum in the Church* (Louisville: Westminster John Knox Press, 1989), chapter 1.

2013, to pray for him. From an ecclesial perspective, this action was a true acknowledgment of the Church as the People of God. From a liturgical perspective, this action was the expression of a praying Church.

As previously noted, several documents of the Second Vatican Council highlight the Church's identity and responsibility to her apostolic and pastoral mission. The periods and steps of the initiation journey of faith make this a reality. I agree with Lawrence Mick, who in 1989 said, "[T]he RCIA offers the best hope we have of becoming a renewed and vibrant Church, the kind of Church envisioned by the Second Vatican Council and, I believe, the kind of Church that the Lord calls us to be."[2] The parish community carries out its baptismal vocation, in a significant way, in and through the *Rite of Christian Initiation of Adults.*

Although much has been written about the role of the community in the RCIA since its 1988 implementation, in practice, the primary importance of the parish community is sometimes forgotten. Today, more than ever, pastoral practice warrants deeper appreciation for the parish's role in initiation. The basis for engaging the parish community in the initiation process can be found by exploring the historical, ecclesial, and liturgical nature of the Church.

A Historical Perspective

As stated in the opening chapters of this book, ancient practice is the backdrop to contemporary initiation practice. At its peak, during the fourth century, the catechumenate was a time for catechumens to share in the life of the Christian community. Those accepted into the catechumenate studied, prayed, and participated in active service to others with members of the community. In other words, catechumens learned a new way of being in the world from those who lived the Gospel in the everyday experiences of their lives. The early Christian community took their Christian lifestyle seriously; therefore, they were the richest resource and practical context for those preparing for initiation.

Sunday, the day of the resurrection, celebrated the risen Christ among his people. Paschal mystery, the death and resurrection of Jesus Christ, became the hope-filled message that gave identity to the Christian

2. Lawrence E. Mick, *RCIA: Renewing the Church as an Initiating Assembly* (Collegeville, MN: Liturgical Press, 1989), 10.

community. The oldest form of catechesis occurred during the homily when the Christian community gathered on Sunday. Significantly, it was through the gathered assembly that faith was handed on. This historical context indicates that catechesis was directed toward the nurture of conversion and rebirth in faith for a paschal way of living.

Ecclesial Perspective

As mentioned earlier, *Lumen gentium* proclaims a renewed awareness of the Church as a community of believers. Significantly, it states, "At all times and in every race, anyone who hears God and does what is right has been acceptable to him (Acts 10:35). He has, however, willed to make men holy and save them, not as individuals without any bond or link between them, but rather to make them into a people who might acknowledge him and serve him in holiness" (LG, 9). Additionally, *Ad gentes* states, "[T]he obligation of spreading the faith falls individually on every disciple of Christ" (AG, 23). Fittingly, the *Rite of Christian Initiation of Adults* clearly affirms, "The initiation of catechumens is a gradual process that takes place within the community of the faithful" (RCIA, 4). Moreover, in the section on ministries and offices, the *Rite of Christian Initiation of Adults* places the role of the community at the forefront. Remarkably, this is the first document to give such high priority to the community—the People of God. And so, the following key paragraph from the rite is worth repeating:

> [T]he people of God, as represented by the local Church, should understand and show by their concern that the initiation of adults is the responsibility of all the baptized. Therefore the community must always be fully prepared in the pursuit of its apostolic vocation to give help to those who are searching for Christ. . . . Hence, the entire community must help the candidates and the catechumens throughout the process of initiation. (RCIA Introduction, 9)

The vision of the Church as a community, rooted in love and mutual concern for the other, is therefore strongly reflected in the *Rite of Christian Initiation of Adults*.

It is also important to remember that the Church views catechumens as part of the "Household of Christ."[3] This statement alone bares with it the responsibility of all members of the household. It implies the richness and splendor that comes with, for example, the expectation and birth of a new baby within a family. In every family the anticipation for and arrival of a new baby is filled with excitement, joy, and hope beyond all measure. In much the same way, the *Rite of Christian Initiation of Adults* is meant to stir such affects.

Undoubtedly, the *Rite of Christian Initiation of Adults* strengthens the vision of the Church grounded in a biblical identity of community. Therefore, as the People of God, we are called to nurture and welcome people into the Household of Christ. In doing so, we too will rediscover the rich meaning of our own identity that is rooted in the sacraments of initiation.

Liturgical Perspective

Theological and pastoral guidelines for liturgy are articulated in *Sacrosanctum concilium*, which envisions liturgy as the source and summit of Christian life (SC, 10). Everything the community is flows from and is directed toward the liturgy, the ritual prayer of the community. Relationship, then, is a key theological aspect of liturgy. For it is the whole Church that participates in the redemption of the world.[4] Vatican II affirms the understanding that rites are performed by and with the community, not for them. Furthermore, liturgy understood as the Church at prayer stirs awareness for this broader meaning of "full, conscious, and active participation" (SC, 14). And, at its deepest level, such participation draws one into the paschal mystery of Christ, made present in the liturgy. On yet another level, active participation implores us to understand the gathered assembly at prayer as revealing the presence of Christ in our midst (SC, 7).

Throughout the process of Christian initiation, the gathered community is a vital part of the formation of the catechumen. In and through

3. See William Harmless, *Augustine and the Catechumenate* (Collegeville, MN: Liturgical Press, 1995).

4. Kevin Irwin, *Context and Text: Method in Liturgical Theology* (Collegeville, MN: Liturgical Press, 1994), 8–9.

the rituals that mark the stages of the catechumen's journey—for example, the Rite of Acceptance into the Order of Catechumens, the rites within the catechumenate proper, the rites celebrated during the Period of Purification and Enlightenment, the sacraments of initiation celebrated at the Easter Vigil, and the Masses for Neophytes during Easter Time—the assembly is never a passive audience watching the ritual action. More accurately, it is in and through the celebration of these liturgical rites that the Church's self-understanding is made manifest. The liturgy, the prayer of the faith community, is the expression of a praying Church and in turn manifests the Church's faith.[5] It must be understood that the *Rite of Christian Initiation of Adults* has the potential to express this reality at a deep level. And it cannot be missed that the gathered assembly, the community of the baptized, actualizes the rich meaning of *lex orandi lex credendi* (as we worship so we believe).

Evangelization: Proclaiming the Life, Death, and Resurrection of Jesus, the Christ

The Period of Evangelization and Precatechumenate which is of great importance, precedes the celebration of the Acceptance into the Order of Catechumens (RCIA, 36). During this period, people inquire about belonging to the Church. In an unhurried period of time (RCIA, 43), the faith community evangelizes by living its faith well and by proclaiming a God that lives in and through Jesus Christ in the Church. Inquirers merit the attention and support of various parish groups, for example, families, priests, deacons, and catechists (RCIA, 38).

Having demonstrated initial faith and a sense of Church and prayer, the inquirer expresses a desire to enter more deeply into a relationship with God and the Church. The Church recognizes this desire and celebrates it ritually. In this regard, the *Rite of Christian Initiation of Adults* states:

> The rite that is called the rite of acceptance into the order of catechumens is of utmost importance. Assembling publicly for the first time, the candidates who have completed the period of the precatechumenate declare their intention to the Church and the Church in turn, *carrying out its apostolic mission*, accepts them as persons who intend to become

5. See Irwin, *Context and Text*.

> its members. God showers his grace on the candidates, since the celebration manifests their desire publicly and marks their reception and first consecration by the Church. (RCIA, 41; emphasis added)

A close look at the above paragraph illustrates that we cannot dismiss the importance of this major step in the lives of those who need to be shown how (by the community) to prayerfully discern the decision to become a catechumen. The willingness, on the part of the community, to share their faith stories in the precatechumenate stage supports the inquirer's desire to know Christ intimately. This is expressed publicly for the first time in the rite of acceptance. In other words, becoming a catechumen is a major step for the inquirer and for the Church. We must always remember that canon laws states: "Catechumens are linked with the Church in a special way since, moved by the Holy Spirit, they are expressing an explicit desire to be incorporated in the Church. By this very desire, as well as by the life of faith, hope and charity which they lead, they are joined to the Church which already cherishes them as its own" (CIC, 206).[6] Implicit within this reality is the responsibility of all the baptized to be invested in the entire process of Christian initiation from the precatechumenate period through mystagogy.

Radical Hospitality

The *Rite of Christian Initiation of Adults* also calls for the entire parish to offer hospitality, and parish hospitality is connected to what the rite tells us in paragraph 9 cited above. In other words, hospitality begins with the parish community. This means that the community is a witness to the Gospel, in every way, and this shines through to the strangers in our midst.

In one parish, it was my experience that many inquirers came to our parish from outside of the parish's geographical boundaries. I would always ask, "What brings you to this parish?" They inevitably answered, "The people here are friendly; the people here are kind; the people in the neighborhood help others; I feel welcomed here!"

Recently, one of my students wanted to know what the RCIA was really about because he did not understand what he saw going on in

6. See John M. Huels, *The Catechumenate and the Law: A Pastoral and Canonical Commentary for the Church in the United States* (Chicago: Liturgy Training Publications, 1994).

parishes. His experience of the RCIA was a set of classes; he could not see how this would change lives. After rich discussion, he realized that, ideally, initiation ministry exhibits radical hospitality. Gratefully, he now understands what his instinct told him, that is, that the parish is called into relationship with people who are seeking to know the Lord.

In light of this, it is imperative to understand that initiation ministers, who represent the parish community, need to show radical hospitality toward inquirers, catechumens, and candidates. They need to be deeply interested in their story, listen to them, and be vulnerable enough to share their story of why, as the baptized, they are committed to staying in the Catholic Church. Significantly, this kind of hospitality is always connected to the Word of God. Like the two disciples on the road to Emmaus, when we invite the stranger to stay, our eyes will be opened to recognize the risen Lord in a deeper way. When we invite the stranger to stay, they begin to feel a sense of belonging to this community and, in particular, how this community and the Christian story makes a difference in their lives; in turn, they make a difference in our lives too.

There is a wisdom to radical hospitality. It is deeply connected to evangelization and in a profound way to Christian identity. Christine Pohl in her beautiful book *Making Room: Rediscovering Hospitality as a Christian Tradition*, writes, "Hospitality is a way of life fundamental to Christian Identity. . . . A mystery of hospitality is how often one senses God's presence in the midst of ordinary activities."[7]

The *Rite of Christian Initiation of Adults*, when fully implemented, helps us to understand this wisdom of true hospitality. The rite clearly recognizes the Church as a community, the Body of Christ, where people care for each other in a radical way. In many ways, at the heart of the rite, there is a recovery of the tradition of hospitality. This sense of hospitality is not new. It goes back to ancient Israel where people knew what it meant to be a stranger on a journey and that they had to be responsible to one another. Jesus, in everything he said and did, demonstrated radical hospitality, especially in his ministry of meal sharing. Keep in mind, for the Jewish people sharing a meal with someone meant they shared life with them. During his public ministry, as we know, Jesus shared meals

7. Christine D. Pohl, *Making Room: Rediscovering Hospitality as a Christian Tradition* (Grand Rapids: Eerdmans, 1999), x, xiii.

with all sorts of people. The Jewish leaders of the time were scandalized by this. It is through his meal sharing, however, that Jesus challenges a narrow view of hospitality. We see this in Scripture, for example:

> When you hold a lunch or dinner, do not invite your friends or your brothers . . . or your wealthy neighbors. . . . Rather, when you hold a banquet, invite the poor, the crippled, the lame, the blind. (Luke 14:12–14)

> For I was hungry and you gave me food, I was thirsty and you gave me drink, *a stranger and you welcomed me*, naked and you clothed me, ill and you cared for me, in prison and you visited me. (Matthew 25:35–36; emphasis added)

Pastoral Implications

The role of the parish community is made known through many innovative ways. One powerful way is that at every Mass, when catechumens are present, the priest can refer to them and make good connections regarding the catechumenate in his homily or introductory remarks. The weekly dismissal, when appropriately understood, poses an opportunity to help catechumens and the baptized gain a deeper sense of identity. In one parish with which I am familiar, the catechumens gather and are seated in a prominent place among the assembly every Sunday. In turn, the dismissal of the catechumens occurs each week. The significance of the dismissal is explained through a recurring bulletin announcement, listed in the worship aid, and accompanied by a familiar sung acclamation. Repeatedly, catechumens articulate a strong sense of prayer and support as they process through a caring community.

All of the rites that take the catechumen through the process of initiation include the assembly. For example, in the Rite of Acceptance into the Order of Catechumens, after the Candidates' First Acceptance of the Gospel (RCIA, 52), there is the Affirmation by the Sponsor and the Assembly (RCIA, 53). The assembly's role is demonstrated by a powerful experience I had several years ago, when, on Holy Saturday morning, after the preparatory rites, a parishioner, unknown to one of the elect, approached him and mentioned how inspired she was by his presence every Sunday and she couldn't wait for him to be initiated that night at the Easter Vigil.

Having explored the role of the community and its importance for the *Rite of Christian Initiation of Adults,* in the next chapter I look at how to recruit the initiation team.

CHAPTER SIX

Recruiting the Initiation Team

Jesus did not tell the apostles to form an exclusive and elite group. He said: "Go and make disciples of all nations" (Mt 28:19).

—*Evangelii gaudium*, 113

After taking a course, "RCIA: Theology and Practice," a talented and enthusiastic student went to her parish coordinator of Christian initiation to offer her services in whatever way she could help. Sadly, the coordinator declined her request, telling her, "We are all set." It is very important to realize that an initiation team is primarily about evangelization. It is not an exclusive group. Initiation ministry is the work of the parish, not a select group, and needs people to tell their story of belonging to the Church and their experience of the action and presence of Christ in their lives.

The initiation team is representative of the parish. In the situation mentioned above it would have been better practice for the coordinator to engage the student in conversation and invite her to discern her gifts for service in the catechumenate. Conversely, my initial experience in this ministry as a sponsor prompted my interest in the rite. The coordinator noticed my enthusiasm and graciously invited me to be the coordinator of the sponsors.

The practice of ministry is vital to the parish that embraces their mission and truly engages in a vision for effective evangelization. This is particularly true for initiation ministry. The question remains, how do we recruit people for the initiation team? Very often, you might hear an announcement or a read a bulletin article requesting volunteer ministers for parish ministries. In my experience, however, this is not an effective practice. When an appeal for volunteers is made in this way, it somehow seems to give the impression that we just want to fill roles rather than give people the opportunity to discern their gifts for service. Remember, in chapter 2, I discussed the importance of discipleship, discernment, vocation, and charisms for the practice of ministry, and in chapter 5, I discussed the indispensable role of the parish community. Both of these chapters allude to the important point that in an evangelizing parish, the call to ministry should be an ongoing aspect of parish life. Therefore, an ongoing parish announcement or bulletin article can provide the parish with information about the *Rite of Christian Initiation of Adults* in general, while at the same time keeping people aware of their responsibility and call to discipleship.

When I was a coordinator of Christian initiation, I made a concerted effort to get to know people though various parish activities. Hospitality Sunday, for example, was a wonderful opportunity to talk informally with parishioners. If I had a sense that someone could bring their gifts and talents to the initiation team, I followed up with them and invited them to consider this ministry and to come and see. You might also ask team members to suggest parishioners they may feel well suited to initiation ministry.

In my view, personal invitation is the most effective way to engage team members. Personal invitation gives people a sense of belonging, confidence, and humility. Nevertheless, if a person comes asking to become involved in initiation ministry, do take the time to speak with them, explain the rite, and the various roles for initiation ministry.

Create Awareness

While ongoing bulletin articles, website announcements, and social media posts are very helpful to keep the parish informed, you might also consider having an information session on discipleship, discernment, and ministry. In relationship to parish stewardship, some parishes hold an annual ministry fair. Practices such as these demonstrate all of the good work being accomplished in the parish and, at the same time, serve as an invitation to ministry.

Several effective strategies can also be found in *Disciples Making Disciples: Print and Digital Resources for Forming the Assembly.* Accommodated to the liturgical year, this resource offers practical information on the dignity of the baptized, an overview of the process of Christian initiation, and an explanation of the periods and steps of the rite. In addition, there are short videos to help inspire the inevitable role of the faithful. You might consider using this helpful tool as a way to keep the parish and initiation team informed about the ongoing ministry of Christian initiation. Valuable and creative information is also provided on how to use the resources on social media, website, email, or as handouts.

Understanding Your Parish

The parish can be described in many ways, but at a basic level, it is a community of the Christian faithful. A more developed theological understanding tells us that the parish is the Body of Christ expressed in a particular locality. In addition, John Paul II's postsynodal apostolic exhortation *Christifideles laici* beautifully states:

> The ecclesial community, while always having a universal dimension, finds its most immediate and visible expression in the parish. . . . In a certain sense it is the Church living in the midst of the homes of her sons and daughters. It is necessary that in light of the faith all rediscover the true meaning of the parish, that is, the place where the very "mystery" of the Church is present and at work. (CL, 26)

Therefore, we can see that the parish is held in high esteem. That being said, it is so important for all parish ministers to do their very best to understand and know the people that make up this sacred community.

Concerning recruiting the initiation team, the coordinator needs to know and understand the people who make up the community. I think we are all aware that, for some time now, cultural diversity has shaped the Catholic Church.[1] Therefore, in recruiting the initiation team, the diversity of the parish must be represented. In addition, cultural

1. Patricia Wittberg, SC, *Catholic Cultures: How Parishes Can Respond to the Changing Face of Catholicism* (Collegeville, MN: Liturgical Press, 2016), 5.

awareness and sensitivity must be a part of the ongoing formation of the team. A helpful resource for this topic is *Building Intercultural Competence for Ministers*, which tells us, "One cannot preach, teach or form persons in the Catholic faith adequately without attending to the ways that Catholic faith and identity become embodied in culture."[2] The same would hold true for those coming to inquire about our faith, and the team would need to understand how to respond to situations, communicate, and build relationships with people who have a different cultural heritage. Team members need to be aware of the different values, behaviors, and artifacts that shape religious beliefs and practice.[3] In addition, they must appreciate that "[t]he presence of brothers and sisters from different cultures should be celebrated as a gift to the Church."[4]

Ongoing Recruitment and a Year-Round Catechumenate

Ed called our parish in July inquiring about becoming Catholic. Baptized in another ecclesial community, for many years he was drawn to the Catholic liturgy. As a professional singer, he had the opportunity to sing in choirs in several Catholic churches. A life-threatening illness compelled him to fulfill his dream of becoming Catholic. He did not geographically live in our parish; in fact, he lived several miles away in another diocese. Sadly, because it was the summer, no one at any of his neighborhood parishes would speak to him. He told me that ours was the last parish he called, and he almost did not make the call thinking that maybe God did not have Catholicism in mind for him.

Because our parish vision for initiation was year-round, I met Ed the next day, and he came to our (ongoing) inquiry session the following week. A few months later, on the Solemnity of Christ the King, he was received into the full communion of the Catholic Church. After his reception, he enthusiastically attended our (year-round) monthly mystagogy

2. *Building Intercultural Competence for Ministers* (Washington, DC: United States Conference for Catholic Bishops, 2011), introduction.

3. Wittberg, *Catholic Cultures*, 2–4.

4. *Welcoming the Stranger among Us: Unity in Diversity* (Washington, DC: United States Catholic Conference, 2000), 3.

sessions and remained an active member of our parish despite the distance from his home.[5]

Year-round means that the parish is prepared, at any time, to welcome an inquirer. It also means that when an unbaptized inquirer discerns readiness for the catechumenate period, we can celebrate Acceptance into the Order of Catechumens (RCIA, 48–74). And, if necessary, we can celebrate this rite more than once during the year (preferably during Ordinary Time).

A year-round model also helps us give the appropriate attention to baptismal status of the inquirer to avoid treating everyone the same. In this regard, it is important to understand what the *National Statutes for the Catechumenate* say:

> The term "catechumen" should be strictly reserved for the unbaptized who have been admitted into the order of catechumens; the term "convert" should be reserved strictly for those converted from unbelief to Christian belief and never be used of those baptized Christians who are received into the full communion of the Catholic Church. (NS, 2)

In other words, as stated throughout this book, for the unbaptized, the *Rite of Christian Initiation of Adults* envisions a gradual process with a catechumenate of at least one year (RCIA, 4 and 75; NS, 6) with the celebration of baptism, confirmation, and Eucharist at the Easter Vigil. On the other hand, baptized Christians, from other ecclesial communities, like Ed, do not need a lengthy period of formation. In fact, we can celebrate Reception into the Full Communion of the Catholic Church (RCIA, 473–98) when the person is ready, anytime during the year, and, if necessary, for one person at a time. Reception into full communion should not take place at the Easter Vigil (NS, 33).

Mary Birmingham expresses the vision for a year-round process, writing:

> Many people have been captivated by the vision of the year-round catechumenate as set forth in the *Rite of Christian Initiation of Adults* (RCIA) but are prevented from proceeding by the seemingly overwhelming and unimaginable challenges of implementing this vision. But appearances

---

5. This story has been told several times throughout my work with the permission of the inquirer.

can be deceiving. Far from being overwhelming and unimaginable, implementing a year-round catechumenate is not only possible, but it is also the best stewardship of the gifts and talents of potential initiation ministers.[6]

A year-round process for celebrating the *Rite of Christian Initiation of Adults* is far less intimidating when you have an ongoing process for recruiting an initiation team. In the next chapter, I recommend that a core team be in place to work with the coordinator. The core team, in turn, could engage coordinators for the various ministries involved for the different periods of the rite. These coordinators could enlist several parishioners to be available, for example, for the precatechumenate, for dismissal, and for extended catechesis so that they could take place all year long. Please note, during the summer months, extended catechesis may look very different. Be creative! Remember, catechesis takes place beyond the scheduled weekly sessions. For example, you might have sponsors invite the catechumens and candidates to their home or to parish social events. The precatechumenate session might take place less often, but team members should be available as needed. In one parish, I had a team of two people who were a phone call away and always available to meet with inquirers.

The key to making this work effectively is to have more than one person fulfilling these roles. The coordinator of Christian initiation should consistently work to build the initiation team. This practice will lessen the burden and prevent ministry burnout. Essentially, in a year-round model, depending on need, precatechumenate, catechumenate, and mystagogy could be going on simultaneously. The only period designated to a particular time is purification and enlightenment, which takes place during the season of Lent.

Implementing a year-round model is a shift away from a practice to which many parishes are accustomed (and many coordinators inherited). Unfortunately, many parishes all but shut down during the summer months. This practice perpetuates a school-year model and effectively communicates to the community that ministry is not a year-round priority. I propose, however, particularly for the *Rite of Christian Initiation of*

6. Mary Birmingham, *Year-Round Catechumenate* (Chicago: Liturgy Training Publications, 2003), 1.

Adults, to move away from this mentality. If, for example, we cease to have the dismissal of the catechumens during the summer months, we are sending the message that this rite and practice are not important. Be considerate and flexible, though, especially when catechumens go on vacation. Just ask them to communicate with you when they will not attend Sunday liturgy. Let them know from the start how important they are and the preparation that goes into the dismissal rite and dismissal catechesis. Catechumenal ministry and the ministerial life of the parish are year-round because evangelization and discipleship are year-round.

The secret to a successful parish is hospitality and, as previously mentioned, this means that we are willing to accompany others and be present to those who desire to be "intentional disciples" willing to serve for the good of the Church's mission.

RCIA Calls for Shared Ministry

As previously stated, the parish community is the primary minister of initiation, and the initiation team is representative of the parish. For full implementation of the rite, however, carried out year-round, specific ministers are needed. The initiation coordinator needs to look to recruit and invite the following:

- **Coordinator of the Precatechumenate:** recruits people from the parish who are available throughout the year to speak with inquirers interested in the Catholic Church. They need to be open, friendly, and willing to meet people where they are. One of the most basic qualities for precatechumenate ministers is their comfort in sharing their story—their experience of following Christ in the Catholic Christian community.
- **Coordinator of Sponsors:** recruits people who will act as companions for catechumens and candidates as they journey toward the sacraments. The most important quality of a sponsor is presence and support.
- **Coordinator of the Catechumenate:** needs a rich understanding of RCIA 75 and have the ability to recruit, train, and accompany catechists for this period.

- **Coordinator of Purification and Enlightenment:** needs to understand fully the profound impact of this period and how it is different from the catechumenate. They need to collaborate with the pastoral staff and recruit people who are good facilitators of prayer, reflection, and retreat planning.
- **Coordinator of Mystagogy:** follows up and invites the neophytes to the Masses for Neophytes (primarily Sunday Mass), as well as scheduling monthly gatherings that will aid in nourishing and supporting them as they are more fully incorporated into the life of the parish.
- **Coordinator of Hospitality:** prepares the environment and recruits others to help with setting up (and cleaning up) light refreshments. They keep an eye on participants to ensure that they are taken care of and feel welcome.
- **Ordained Ministers:** this is the role of the priests and deacons of the parish. They should become comfortable with the ritual text, its language and nuances. They should also occasionally be invited to attend precatechumenate and catechumenate sessions to become acquainted with participants. They need to be available to catechumens and candidates who might need help with discernment and require spiritual direction.[7]
- **Musicians:** the coordinator needs to collaborate with the parish musicians when preparing the rites. In addition, they might be invited to a session not only to meet participants but also to provide music for prayer and reflection.
- **Prayer leaders:** the coordinator might look to parish prayer groups for people to lead prayer and facilitate reflection.

As you can see, an initiation team involves a variety of talents. Look to the wider parish community, create an awareness for initiation ministry, and invite people to come and see the extraordinary treasure that lies deep within the RCIA. The final chapter of this book will provide suggestions for the training and formation of the initiation team.

---

7. The coordinator may also recommend and encourage a catechumen or candidate to regularly work with a lay spiritual director.

Preventing Ministry Burnout

> *Then Moses again had recourse to the LORD and said, "LORD, why have you treated this people badly? And why did you send me? From the time I went to Pharaoh to speak on your name, he has treated this people badly, and you have done nothing to rescue your people." (Exodus 5:22–23)*
>
> *All the Israelites did exactly as the LORD had commanded Moses and Aaron. On that same day the LORD brought the Israelites out of the land of Egypt company by company. (Exodus 12:50–51)*

Scripture scholars say that the Book of Exodus presents the tension between hope and despair. Theologian William Willimon says:

> This same tension between hope and despair, failure and victory—tension that is at the heart of the biblical story—continues to be at the heart of church life today. . . . Some days we are Moses standing in despair before the bickering, faithless children of Israel. On other days, we are Moses arguing with God, refusing to prophesy, unsure of ourselves and the power of God. There are still other days that we are part of the amazing liberation of God.[8]

Willimon also explains, "Burnout is a term borrowed from rocketry. It denotes a lack of energy when a rocket, soaring upward, runs out of fuel and falls back to earth."[9] In recent years, burnout is a term that has taken on meaning concerning the human condition and refers to frustration, apathy, overwork, or stress. In *Ministry Burnout* John A. Sanford states: "Burnout is a word we use when a person has become exhausted with his or her profession or major life activity."[10] Sanford goes on to say that a "ministering person" can be prone to burnout. He cites several reasons for this. For example, ministry is ongoing, repetitive, holds expectation, often lacks satisfaction, and drains one's energy.[11] As parish staffs decrease in number, burnout is a real threat to ministry.

---

8. William H. Willimon, *Clergy and Laity Burnout* (Nashville: Abingdon Press, 1989), 19.
9. Willimon, *Clergy and Laity Burnout*, 21.
10. John A. Sanford, *Ministry Burnout* (New York: Paulist Press, 1982), 1.
11. Sanford, *Ministry Burnout*, 5–16.

Good leadership on the part of the initiation coordinator and consistently following the suggestions for ongoing recruitment can help alleviate the experience of ministry burnout. One of the most important things to keep in mind is that no one person can or should do initiation ministry. The background provided in the opening chapters of this book call for relational and collaborative ministry. In other words, ministry is people working together as true disciples. When this type of ministry is set in motion, the profound meaning of initiation ministry will provide the energy needed, and there will be no lack of commitment to the catechumens, candidates, elect, and neophytes.

Ministry burnout will be a thing of the past when, as true disciples of Jesus Christ, we keep the fire burning with meaning, mission, and motivation. When, however, on a human level, we see the fire dimming in a particular person, we might need to ask what circumstances are contributing to and fostering burnout. Everyone, at one time or another, goes through a trial of sorts. Some may need a leave of absence from ministry. Whatever the case may be, the human reality of burnout calls us to deepen the spiritual formation for the initiation team. Retreat, reflection, and prayer hold the power to refresh the spirit and, at the same time, revitalize the work of the initiation team. The coordinator should make certain to provide opportunities for the initiation team to step away for time of recollection in order to renew their own conversion and encounter with the Trinity. "If ministry does not flow from a personal encounter and ongoing relationship with the Lord, then no matter how 'accomplished' it may be in its methods and activities, that ministry will lack the vital soul and source needed to bear lasting fruit."[12]

Once the work of ongoing recruitment becomes part of parish practice, the next chapter looks at the needs of the parish and explores how to best develop an initiation team.

12. *Co-Workers*, 38.

CHAPTER SEVEN

Developing the Initiation Team

Chapter 5 looked at the primacy of the role of the parish community in Christian initiation. It is important to realize that the initiation team represents the community and provides a service within the context of the parish community. In the last chapter, I looked at team recruitment. This chapter focuses on developing an initiation team. It looks at the vital role of the coordinator of Christian initiation and the role of the initiation team who work together, not only to facilitate the rite, but also to animate the parish in an appreciation for the rite and its highly effective impact on the entire parish. Keep in mind, the development of an initiation team is certainly determined by the needs of the parish; the principles set forth here can be adapted to your parish.

The Coordinator of Initiation Ministry

The coordinator of Christian initiation plays a vital role in the full implementation of the *Rite of Christian Initiation of Adults*. Sometimes the coordinator is a member of the pastoral staff, or perhaps they are a volunteer appointed by the pastor. In either case, the coordinator must first and foremost understand the *Rite of Christian Initiation of Adults* with all of its nuance.[1] It is my recommendation that the coordinator fully understand part 1 of the rite; only then can they make the adaptations present in part 2. The coordinator must be well prepared to provide pastoral care to inquirers, catechumens, candidates, and neophytes and, at the same time, empower a support team to help facilitate this effectively.

Another important aspect of being the coordinator is the ability to collaborate with the pastor, priests, deacons, liturgist, music director, coordinator of the lectors, hospitality ministers, and ushers, especially

1. For a basic commentary on the RCIA, see Eschenauer, *The Role of the Coordinator in Christian Initiation*.

when preparing the rites. In addition, it is important to stay connected with other initiation coordinators in the diocese and be well informed about diocesan guidelines, available workshops, publications, and new resources. The coordinator of Christian initiation should be the resource person for the pastoral staff as well as the one, with the support of the initiation team, who animates and informs the entire parish about the *Rite of Christian Initiation of Adults*.

For some, initiation ministry may seem complex, even daunting. As mentioned above, the rite is designed to be the work of the entire parish; however, it is a ministry that is overseen and facilitated by the coordinator, with the help of an initiation team. The coordinator should set a schedule of team meetings, perhaps at intervals during the year-round precatechumenate and catechumenate, before a celebration of the rite of acceptance into the catechumenate, before the rite of election, before the Easter Vigil, and during Easter Time. Team meetings should include, for example, prayer and reflection, evaluation of the process and participants, ongoing study of the RCIA ritual text, reflection on the Word of God, reflection on the liturgical year.

The Initiation Team

The initiation team is a group of faithful parishioners who represent the parish community. The size of the team may be determined by the size of the parish. In a large parish a core support team may be formed that would consist of, for example, the coordinator of Christian initiation, a priest, a deacon, coordinator of sponsors, coordinator of catechists, coordinator of dismissal sessions, and coordinator of hospitality. In turn, this core support team would recruit and form sponsors, catechists, facilitators of dismissal catechesis, and hospitality ministers. In a smaller parish an initiation team consisting of the coordinator, priest, deacon, sponsors, catechists, facilitators, and hospitality minister could work together effectively. The main thing to realize is that initiation ministry should not be done by one person. It is especially important to realize that it should not be the sole responsibility of the pastor or any one priest. Initiation ministry is, first and foremost, the role of the parish; however, as previously mentioned, the initiation team acts as parish representatives who work to organize and facilitate the periods and steps of the rite.

The initiation team consists of people who are willing to share their story of living the Christian life and, at the same time, introduce inquirers, catechumens, candidates, and neophytes to the parish community. They can do this very effectively with appropriate human, spiritual, pastoral, and intellectual formation (chapter 3).

Two Possible Scenarios for Team Development

I. Developing a New Team

If your parish is just beginning to implement the *Rite of Christian Initiation of Adults*, developing a new team can be very exciting. Some parishes may want to have the team in place before they start full implementation. If, for example, you have not implemented the rite and do not have catechumens, you could spend up to a year preparing the team for initiation ministry. In this case a good way to start is with a small core support team —a group of five or six dedicated parishioners who are open and eager to learning about the *Rite of Christian Initiation of Adults*.

Once you have identified possible parishioners for the core team invite them to an initial session. For planning sessions with the team, a helpful resource is *Guide for Training Initiation Ministers: An Introduction to the RCIA* by Michael Ruzicki. This resource is a companion to Ron Lewinski's *An Introduction to the RCIA: The Vision of Christian Initiation*. Ruzicki's book consists of ten training sessions for initial and ongoing team formation on the Church's vision for Christian initiation.

Begin by welcoming participants and thanking them for their time and willingness to learn about initiation ministry. Briefly explain the purpose of the meeting—that is, an introduction to the *Rite of Christian Initiation of Adults*. Be sure to provide each participant with a copy of the ritual text (study edition). You could use session one from *Guide for Training Initiation Ministers*, which begins with prayer and then takes the group through the vision of the rite.

One of the most important things, from the start, is to be clear about what the *Rite of Christian Initiation of Adults* is and what it is not. Use the information from chapter 1 of this book to explain the Church's vision of the rite.

Once a core team is in place you will eventually need to expand on it to include catechists, sponsors, facilitators for dismissal catechesis, hospitality ministers, and ideally subteams for the precatechumenate, purification and enlightenment, and mystagogy.

II. Working with an Existing Team

In two different parishes, it was my experience that an initiation team was in place when I came in as a new coordinator. I found that the best thing was to enter into a relationship with the team, become acquainted with them and begin by understanding their gifts and talents and the role they play in the process. Observe how the periods and steps of the rite are currently implemented. If, for example, the rite is implemented on a school-year model, in time, help the team to realize the value of a year-round catechumenate. If the dismissal of catechumens from Mass, especially on Sundays, is not the practice of the parish, first, work with the pastor to explain the value of the dismissal rite for the catechumens and the parish. Then, share this information with the initiation team so that they understand its meaning. It is always important to use the ritual text to help the team better understand the ideal vision for Christian initiation.

Collaboration

Throughout this work, I have mentioned several times that the coordinator of Christian initiation works in collaboration with the initiation team and other ministers of the parish. The work of establishing a parish vision for Christian initiation requires the collaborative efforts of many. Just as we discovered that a rationale for ministry could be found in St. Paul's first letter to the Corinthians, the foundation for the ideal of collaboration can also be found here:

> There are different kinds of spiritual gifts but the same spirit; there are different forms of service but the same Lord; there are different workings but the same God who produces all of them in everyone. To each individual the manifestation of the Spirit is given for some benefit. (1 Corinthians 12:4–7)

This Scripture passage illustrates the relational model for ministry described earlier in this book. In this model the coordinator and the initiation team work with the pastor, priests, deacons, and other ministers in mutual dialogue and respect. In other words, initiation ministers should not work in isolation. They need to effectively implement the *Rite of Christian Initiation of Adults* in collaboration with others. The next chapter will explore the various roles of the initiation team as well as helpful skills and necessary qualities for good and effective initiation ministry.

CHAPTER EIGHT

Formation for Initiation Ministry

In the last chapter, I looked at how you might develop an initiation team in your parish. Once you develop the team, care and time must be taken to adequately form and train the team. Team members need to be willing to gather, reflect, pray, and learn in a joyful and respectful atmosphere. Their formation should integrate the human, spiritual, intellectual, and pastoral formation described in chapter 3. This type of formation will help team members communicate on various levels with each other as well as with inquirers, catechumens, candidates, the elect, and neophytes.

The initiation team must take the following matters seriously:

- Committing to the Church and its teachings
- Understanding the vision of the *Rite of Christian Initiation of Adults*
- Understanding the principles of liturgy
- Understanding the liturgical year
- Appreciating the sacraments of initiation in their lives
- Witnessing to their own faith journey
- Articulating their spiritual journey
- Developing a liturgical spirituality
- Making the liturgical year and lectionary a part of their everyday experience
- Offering radical hospitality
- Engaging in holy listening and the art of accompaniment

Once a team is in place, responsibilities can be delegated with select individuals to coordinate hospitality, sponsors, and catechists for both dismissal catechesis and extended catechesis. In the appendix of this book, you will find more concrete ideas to guide coordinators with team formation.

Coordinator of Hospitality

In chapter 5, I expressed the fact that hospitality is the responsibility of the entire parish. While this is true, it is very important that hospitality be the hallmark of the entire initiation team. More specifically, there could be one or two persons who are responsible for ensuring that a hospitable atmosphere is created for precatechumenate and catechumenate sessions. A coordinator of hospitality can engage others to help with setting up the environment and offering light refreshments. This is a wonderful way to include parishioners in the process. In addition to providing a comfortable environment, hospitality ministers need to be friendly and inviting and, in turn, make the participants feel welcome. Whether the meetings are in a home or at the parish, be sure to welcome participants at the door and ensure that the location for the meeting is easy to find. The meeting space should reflect a prayerful atmosphere. Seating can be around a table or chairs set up in a circle. Create a focal point in the room with a prayer table covered with a cloth reflecting the color for the liturgical season, place a lectionary at the center, and light a candle at the start of the session. Seasonal liturgical music can also help set the tone.

Coordinator of Sponsors

According to the *Rite of Christian Initiation of Adults*, "A sponsor accompanies any candidate seeking admission as a catechumen. Sponsors are people who have known and assisted the candidates and stand witness to the candidates' moral character, faith, and intention" (RCIA Introduction, 10). Simply stated, accompaniment means being present to another. Sponsors in the RCIA are present to help catechumens and candidates ponder and express their encounter with Jesus Christ. In addition, helping participants feel welcome and secure in a new place can make a difference in their experience. Pope Francis places high priority on the "art of accompaniment." He writes:

> In our world, ordained and other pastoral workers can make present the fragrance of Christ's closeness and his personal gaze. The Church will have to initiate everyone—priests, religious, and laity—into this "art of accompaniment" which teaches us to remove our sandals before the sacred ground of the other. The pace of the accompaniment must be steady and reassuring, reflecting our closeness and our compassionate gaze which also heals, liberates and encourages growth in the Christian life. (EG, 169)

Therefore, the sponsor walks with another person, is present to them, and accepts them where they are in their strengths, struggles, challenges, doubts, and joys. This also means that they offer support and encouragement with patience, understanding, and holy listening.

The sponsor begins their ministry with the candidate's acceptance into the catechumenate. Ideally, a sponsor is a member of the parish, but some sponsors may be friends who are not members of the parish or who the team has chosen and pared with the candidate. For example, during the precatechumenate you might watch to see if an inquirer bonds with a particular person. In either case, the sponsor must be willing to get to know the catechumen and accompany them throughout the process.

What is important to understand is that initiation, as I have stated throughout this book, happens in the community, and the initiation team represents the community. In much the same way, then, the sponsor represents the team and works directly with the catechumen during the initiation process and quite possibly beyond.

The formation of sponsors should include an understanding of the rites, appreciating the baptismal vocation, recognizing faith as a journey, appreciating the liturgy, loving Jesus and the Church, respecting relationships, and desiring to invest quality time for another.

On a practical level, it may be helpful, as mentioned in the last chapter, to appoint a coordinator of sponsors on the core team. The coordinator of the sponsors could always be on the lookout for potential sponsors and perhaps form a "pool of sponsors." They could work with interested people in helping them understand the rite as well as the responsibilities of a sponsor. A very helpful resource is *Guide for Sponsors*, fourth edition. Here, Ronald Lewinski reiterates, "It is the role of the sponsor then, together with other members of the parish community, to create a milieu that will be conducive for the dynamics of conversion and passing on our faith tradition."[1]

Coordinator of Catechists

The *Rite of Christian Initiation of Adults* is a rite that engages catechesis and makes actual the liturgical-catechetical relationship. First, catechesis in the catechumenate period needs to be understood in the broad sense. In other words, it is true that catechesis takes place during specific sessions, but it is also true that catechesis takes place in and through various parish activities, especially the Liturgy of the Word on Sunday. This is a concept that should not be overlooked. Catechumens can also learn what it means to be a Catholic Christian by, for example, attending the parish picnic or working in the food pantry. In this regard, be attentive to making sure they are invited to these activities.

Regarding the formation of catechists, first, it is important to realize that there are two types of catechetical sessions, commonly known as dismissal catechesis and extended catechesis. Dismissal catechesis is for catechumens and actually begins in the liturgical assembly and starts with the Liturgy of the Word and dismissal rite. Extended catechesis, as you will see, is centered on the Liturgy of the Word and focuses on a particular doctrine that is drawn from the Sunday readings. Extended catechesis may take place on Sunday, after the dismissal catechesis, or on an alternative day or evening. The most important aspect of being a catechist is to understand and internalize what the rite says about the catechumenate period. RCIA, paragraph 75 provides key aspects for catechesis: catechesis is accommodated to the liturgical year. This means that the liturgy, the liturgical year, and the lectionary are the sources for catechesis, and catechesis is rooted in the life of the community. In other words, people become familiar with Christian life through the prayer and support of sponsors and the entire parish community. Catechesis also takes place through liturgical rites. We see this specifically in the section "Rites Belonging to the Period of the Catechumenate," which includes Celebrations of the Word of God (RCIA, 81–89); Minor Exorcisms (RCIA, 90–94); Blessings of the Catechumens (RCIA, 95–97); and Anointing

1. Ronald J. Lewinski, *Guide for Sponsors*, 4th ed. (Chicago: Liturgy Training Publications, 2008), 15.

of the Catechumens (RCIA, 98–103). Catechesis also takes place when the catechumens engage in service. They should be formed to understand that service is a way of life that is rooted in the Gospel.

Very importantly, paragraph 75 affirms the liturgy-catechetical relationship and demonstrates that the liturgy itself forms and shapes the catechumen. The language of the liturgy, the prayers, the actions, the gestures, and the symbols, express what ordinary words cannot. Liturgy, in a sense, is the first catechism! Let's take a practical look at what catechesis in the catechumenate might look like.

Dismissal Catechesis

Beginning with Acceptance into the Order of Catechumens and continuing until the celebration of the sacraments of initiation, catechumens gather with the faithful for the Sunday Liturgy of the Word and are dismissed after the homily, before the universal prayer and the Creed. Paragraph 75.3 says that catechumens, "when they are present in the assembly of the faithful . . . should be kindly dismissed." It is important to realize that catechesis essentially begins in the liturgical assembly, where they learn what it means to gather as the People of God, to pray the liturgy, and, very importantly, to listen attentively to Sacred Scripture.

The dismissal of the catechumens is an important ritual moment. It is a sign of identity, both for the catechumens and for the gathered assembly of the baptized.[2] The dismissal ritual, first, gives the catechumens a better sense of who they are in relationship to the Church. Second, it tells the assembly that there are people in our midst who desire to be baptized. In addition, it should provoke the baptized to consider why we get to stay.

The catechumens are dismissed to continue the Liturgy of the Word while the Mass continues with the Liturgy of the Eucharist.

For dismissal catechesis, the catechist is someone who is a facilitator of prayer and reflection. Their training would include guidance in using resources like, for example, *The Living Word: Leading RCIA Dismissals*, which is available for years A, B, and C. The dismissal catechesis only takes about thirty minutes or so (usually until the end of Mass). You might

2. Please note the baptized includes candidates for full communion in the Catholic Church, who are not dismissed from the Eucharistic liturgy.

then have sponsors and other team members join the catechumens for refreshments.

In preparing for the session, the facilitator reflects on the particular Sunday, season, or feast; reflects on the readings; and considers some themes from the hymns, homily, and readings. Once they arrive at the designated space, the catechist can refocus the group with a hymn or prayer. Then, they would help the catechumens reflect on what they saw, heard, and experienced during the Liturgy of the Word. Catechumens would be encouraged to articulate how God is present in the Word and reflect on the deeper meaning of the Word in their life. Also, using *The Living Word* as a guide, the catechist might ask questions about the readings or the particular Sunday. The session ends with a summary of what was shared or discussed; it then concludes with a prayer.

Extended Catechesis

Dismissal catechesis leads to an extended session, which gets to the heart of the four aspects of catechesis mentioned in RCIA, paragraph 75, which says catechesis is accommodated to the liturgical year, is supported by the community, includes liturgical rites, and engages in apprenticeship in the mission of the Church. It is worth noting, "This catechesis leads the catechumens not only to an appropriate acquaintance with dogmas and precepts but also to a profound sense of the mystery of salvation in which they desire to participate" (RCIA, 75.1). This statement clears up any confusion about catechesis in the catechumenate. It does not negate the teaching of dogmas and precepts. Because catechesis is accommodated to the liturgical year, however, it is the lectionary that determines the topic for catechesis. There are resources available to help the catechist prepare for extended catechesis, for example, *Foundations in Faith*, which is available for years A, B, and C. *The Homiletic Directory* is another helpful resource for catechesis, specifically appendix 1, "The Homily and the Catechism of the Catholic Church." This section of the directory expresses the bond between the homily and the doctrine of the Church and recognizes that doctrine is found deep within Scripture (160). This is significant to catechesis in the catechumenate. Appendix 1 provides a table that lists every Sunday and holyday for all three years of the liturgical cycle with corresponding paragraphs and themes from the *Catechism of the Catholic Church*.[3]

In view of what has already been said, particularly concerning RCIA, 75, the formation for catechists in the catechumenate must be focused on liturgical catechesis. Liturgical catechesis acknowledges that liturgy is the first source for catechesis. Liturgy as the primary source for catechesis is reclaimed and affirmed in the *Catechism of the Catholic Church* and in many catechetical documents, for example, *Catechesi tradendae, General Directory for Catechesis, National Directory for Catechesis,* and *Our Hearts Were Burning within Us.*

Liturgical catechesis is also a very traditional form of catechesis. As mentioned earlier, in the early Church liturgy and catechesis were two sides of the same coin. Interestingly, in the early part of the twentieth century, Benedictine monk Virgil Michel (1890–1938) sought to provide catechesis that was rooted in the Church's liturgy. Virgil Michel worked tirelessly to show that, in his time, catechesis was completely separate from the liturgy, and he insisted that liturgy is the heart of all catechesis. As envisioned in the *Rite of Christian Initiation of Adults*, Virgil Michel's vision for catechesis has become a reality.

The liturgical-catechetical relationship affects all catechetical efforts. The *National Directory for Catechesis* firmly attests, "In the Church's mission of evangelization, catechesis and Liturgy are intimately connected" (NDC, p. 33). In order for this to work effectively, catechists need to be formed according to RCIA, 75. Therefore, formation for catechists includes the following principles:

- The framework for catechesis is the feasts and seasons of the liturgical year.
- Content is centered on the lectionary and liturgical texts found in the Church's rites.
- The liturgical year tells us something about who we are as Christians and who we are to become; it reveals and invites us into the paschal mystery.

3. Donna M. Eschenauer, "Shaping a Living, Active Faith," *Pastoral Liturgy* 47, no. 2 (March/April 2016): 21–23.

- Reflection on the Sunday readings is an important practice for all people.
- Reflection on ritual action reveals how powerful this nonverbal form of catechesis can be.
- Liturgical catechesis is a lifelong process of mystagogy.
- The parish community and the liturgy is the context for catechesis.

Initial and Ongoing Team Formation

It is important to point out that, for team members, initial and ongoing formation should be given high priority. Initial formation focuses on the practice of ministry, pastoral skills, the vision of the *Rite of Christian Initiation of Adults*, and knowledge of the *Catechism of the Catholic Church*. Ongoing formation can be designed to help team members develop their own sense of being a Catholic Christian in the world and a deepening of their spiritual life. A retreat or a day of recollection for the team, for example, may be a good way to foster this. The team also needs to continue to enhance their pastoral skills, which includes leadership skills, ministerial skills, and theological reflection. Intellectual formation nourishes the human, spiritual, and pastoral aspects of ministry. Theological understanding provides wisdom for engaging the Gospel with the secular worldview that is so predominate in the world today. Theological study enhances ministerial skills and helps integrate it into our ministry and our everyday living. In the end, a team that is formed well will bring a prophetic stance to others, fostering hope and confidence in the only thing that matters, an encounter with Jesus Christ that leads to faith, hope, and love—the virtues that are the heart of the spiritual life. In addition, in my experience, it was a healthy pastoral practice to bring the initiation team together socially once or twice a year to share a meal. This can be done by having a simple potluck supper at the parish or in someone's home. This type of hospitality demonstrates a very real pastoral practice. In order for an initiation team to relate and minister to inquirers, catechumens, candidates, and neophytes, members of the team need to be able to relate and minister applicably with each other.

Epilogue

For over thirty years, parishes have been working diligently to implement the *Rite of Christian Initiation of Adults*, and, for the most part, it has proved to be a rich experience. But in many places, the rite has yet to be fully implemented or accurately understood. Reasons for this vary; however, in the end, a parish that neglects to renew its initiation practices neglects to renew its own self-understanding and potential for faith development. The pages of this book attempted to show you that good insight into the practice of ministry, along with an appropriate understanding of the *Rite of Christian Initiation of Adults*, has the potential to transform parish practice.

The vision set forth here can become a reality when the coordinator of Christian initiation, in collaboration with an initiation team, represents the parish in its responsibility for the implementation of the rite. While this is a tremendous task that demands liturgical, catechetical, and pastoral skills, as emphasized through this book, it is equally important that the parish at large also develop an understanding of their role and responsibility to the catechumenate. The initiation team must resist the temptation to take possession of the rite. It is imperative that the assembly is made aware of its role in initiation ministry.

A parish that lives out its mission well and has a clear vision for initiation ministry will inevitably draw new members. A parish that practices radical hospitality and takes the art of accompaniment seriously is well prepared to hand on its values and way of life.

The *Rite of Christian Initiation of Adults* reintroduced us to the Order of Catechumens. Help your parish to understand the importance of this order in the life of the Church. We now recognize the Order of the Faithful, the Order of Presbyter, and the Order of Deacons. People will be delighted to know this. It is fundamental to the life of the Church and the understanding of membership.

The parish that invests time, care, reflection, and personnel for the implementation for the *Rite of Christian Initiation of Adults* makes an investment in the life of the Church. Every facet of the rite provides an opportunity to strengthen who we are as a people called and gifted by God. The theology and ecclesiology woven throughout the rite holds the potential to not only form catechumens but also re-form the baptized, so that they can recover a deeper sense of living out their baptismal vocation. Recovery of a baptismal spirituality, as a vocation to be lived, is vital for our time. It recognizes the baptized as God's light in a darkened world. Entrance into the waters of baptism is entrance into communion with God and one another.

Inclusive, collaborative implementation of the *Rite of Christian Initiation of Adults* is reflective of an art form. Expert pastoral practice and prayerful contemplation are comparable to any artistic work. This calls us to relinquish a program mentality and trust in the power of God's presence and action within the parish community. The rite sets in motion a people, re-formed and renewed for the work of evangelization.

This book is an invitation for you to take a second look at how the *Rite of Christian Initiation of Adults* is implemented in your parish. It calls you to a more fruitful vision of initiation ministry. May your parish community continue to grow and mature in the desire to be a life-giving force for those who thirst for the living God—active and present in all of life.

Appendix

Sample Team Meetings

- Initial and ongoing team meetings can incorporate the dimensions of formation discussed in chapter 3: human, spiritual, pastoral, and intellectual.
- General team meetings, with the core support team, sponsors, and catechists, ought to be scheduled regularly. Once a month may be a reasonable timeframe; however, adapt this timeframe for your parish.
- Team meetings, in general, show that team members are supported and valued for their ministry.
- Team meetings nurture and nourish team members on the human, spiritual, intellectual, and pastoral levels.

Planning the meeting: Initiation coordinators should schedule meetings in advance; then, notify team members of the day, time, and place. Meetings may be held at the parish or in a home. If held at the parish make sure you request the space in advance.

Prepare the space: Whether in a home or in the parish facility, the environment should be prepared ahead of the meeting. Tables and chairs or chairs set up in a circle are conducive for training and discussion. Enhance the space by having a lectionary or Bible in full view, a candle, a table covering that reflects the color for the liturgical season, and video and music equipment.

Handouts: All team members should be provided with the ritual text *Rite of Christian Initiation of Adults, Study Edition.* If you have handouts for the meetings, have them prepared ahead of time and ready to give participants before the meeting begins. If possible, have all materials arranged in a folder with each participant's name on it. This makes it easier as people gather.

Hospitality: Have light refreshments prepared so that as people gather they can socialize before the meeting begins.

Prayer: All meetings should open and close with prayer and reflection. This will enhance the spiritual dimension of ministry formation (*Co-Workers*, Spiritual Formation, p. 38–41). One suggestion is to have a short Liturgy of the Word using the Scripture of the day or the Scripture readings for the following Sunday.

- Begin the prayer with music; consult your parish music director for suggestions on music that will be used in the parish.
- Gather the group with an opening prayer and then have a participant proclaim the reading; provide a period of silence and then have some questions for reflection prepared and allow for sharing; include intercessions and a closing prayer.

Core Support Team Meeting

Who Is Included?

The coordinator is the facilitator of the meeting; depending on your parish, participants may include the pastor or one of the parish priests, a deacon, the coordinator of hospitality, the coordinator of the sponsors, the coordinator of the catechists, the coordinator of the precatechumenate, the coordinator of mystagogy.

Setting the Agenda

a. Prayer.

b. Discussion and observation on process in general; progress or concerns about catechumens, candidates, elect, or neophytes.

c. Topic: "Ministry and the Call to Holiness"; presentation given by coordinator using the material in chapter 2 of this book.

d. Demonstrate how each minister can improve their pastoral and leadership skills. For example, provide information about listening skills or emphasize the importance of presence to others (*Co-Workers*, Pastoral Formation, p. 47–49).

e. Allow for reports on each aspect of ministry (precatechumenate, sponsors, catechists, hospitality, mystagogy, etc.).

f. Look ahead to upcoming events, for example, Acceptance into the Order of Catechumens, Rite of Election, Scrutinies, etc. Whatever the case may be, make this an opportunity for intellectual formation with regard to the rite. Using the ritual text, apply a rites-based approach and provide meaning centered on the prayers, symbols, and gestures of the rite.

g. Give team members the opportunity to express their own ministerial concerns; affirm and critique them, giving them feedback on what you observe. Encourage them to care for themselves and be conscious of a well-balanced behavior for their personal sake and for the sake of their ministry (Co-Workers, Human Formation, p. 36–37).

h. Closing Prayer.

i. Refreshments.

Catechist Meeting

Who Is Included?

This meeting is facilitated by the coordinator of the catechists. Catechists for dismissal and extended catechesis are invited to attend.

Setting the Agenda

a. Prayer and reflection.

b. Discussion and observation on extended catechetical sessions.

c. Topic: "Liturgical Catechesis"; presentation given by the coordinator of the catechists using the material from chapter 8 of this book.

d. Upcoming schedules are provided.

e. Provide catechists the opportunity to ask questions, express concerns, or share observations.

f. Closing prayer.

g. Refreshments and hospitality.

A Guide to Team Formation for Coordinators

(corresponds with chapter 8)

- Commitment to the Church and its teachings
  - a. Explore the *Catechism of the Catholic Church.*
    - i. universal document
    - ii. purpose is to preserve and make clear our Catholic faith
    - iii. profession of faith; celebration of the Christian Mystery; life in Christ (morality); Christian prayer

- Understanding the vision of the *Rite of Christian Initiation of Adults*
  - a. All team members should have a copy of the ritual text (study edition).
  - b. Use the resource *Guide for Training Initiation Ministers: An Introduction to the RCIA.*
  - c. Before each of the rites is celebrated gather the team to reflect on that particular ritual step.

- Understanding the principles of liturgy
  - a. Introduce the team to the liturgy documents.
  - b. Explore and discuss key liturgical principals, for example, the role of the assembly and active participation.
  - c. Explore the resource *Signs and Symbols of the Liturgy: An Experience of Ritual and Catechesis.*

- Understanding the liturgical year
  - a. Have a team meeting that focuses on the meaning of the liturgical year; for reference use the document *Universal Norms on the Liturgical Year and the General Roman Calendar.*
  - b. Help the team to understand the significance of the liturgical year for our identity as Catholic Christians.
  - c. Have a liturgical calendar in view at all times.
  - d. Set the environment for meetings so they reflect the liturgical season.

- Appreciating the sacraments of initiation in their lives
    a. Reflect on the meaning of each of the sacraments of initiation.
    b. Discuss the relevance of these sacraments for their everyday lives.
    c. Pay particular attention to the centrality of the Eucharist in our lives and the idea of living out our baptismal vocation.

- Witnessing to their own faith journey
    a. Provide the opportunity for team members to articulate their faith journey.
    b. Explore the idea of ongoing conversion.

- Articulating their spiritual journey
    a. Provide days or evenings of retreat/recollection.
    b. Incorporate the opportunity for prayer at every team meeting.
    c. Encourage team members to seek spiritual direction.

- Developing a liturgical spirituality
    a. Help team members understand that we live out the liturgy every day, that our thoughts and actions should reflect liturgical prayer.

- Making the liturgical year and lectionary a part of their everyday experience
    a. Celebrate the Liturgy of the Word with team members.
    b. Use the model of "Breaking open the Word" and *lectio divina.*

- Offering radical hospitality
    a. Hospitality begins with the parish community.
    b. Hospitality is connected to evangelization.
    c. The community/team is a witness to the Gospel.
    d. Team members must show sincere interest in the stories told by inquirers, catechumens, candidates, the elect, and neophytes.
    e. Inquirers, catechumens, etc. should always have a sense of feeling welcomed.

- Engaging in holy listening and the art of accompaniment
    a. Team members must demonstrate a true sense of listening: listening to the other without thinking about how they will respond.
    b. This kind of listening is prayerful and reflects a spirit of sacred trust.
    c. Team members are committed to be present to inquirers, catechumens, etc.; they are willing to open their homes to them, share in refreshment or a meal, extend an invitation for them to call or text.

- Unpack the rich social doctrine of the Church
    a. Life and Dignity of the Human Person
    b. Call to Family, Community, and Participation
    c. Rights and Responsibilities
    d. Option for the Poor and Vulnerable
    e. Dignity of Work and Rights of Workers
    f. Solidarity
    g. Care for God's Creation

Model for Celebrating the Dismissal on Sunday

For the dismissal of the catechumens, practically speaking, the celebrant invites the catechumens to come forward. In these or similar words, he should say, "Catechumens, please come forward." I highly recommend that the invitation not say, "Those involved in the RCIA, come forward." This type of invitation treats the catechumens as outsiders and reinforces a "program" mentality of the ritual process. The invitation to the catechumens, who are ordered within the assembly, is important because it grounds their identity as a part of the parish community. After the invitation for catechumens to come forward, RCIA, 67B offers a helpful dismissal formula, which may be adapted.[1] It says:

> My dear friends, this community now sends you forth to reflect more deeply upon the word of God which you have shared with us today. Be assured of our loving support and prayers for you. We look forward to the day when you will share fully in the Lord's Table.

As the catechumens come forth, one catechist accompanies them. The lectionary is presented to the catechist, who leads the catechumens forth in procession while the assembly sings an acclamation as a sign of their prayer and support.

The catechumens need to be taught that they are going to continue the Liturgy of the Word. Therefore, the catechist and catechumens should proceed reverently and quietly to a designated room that is set up for prayer and reflection.

1. Besides *The Living Word* (LTP), which provides a sample dismissal formula, these two resources provide elaborated sample formularies for dismissals: *Sunday Dismissals for the RCIA* by Mary K. Milne, OSU, foreword by Maria Marek, IWBS (Liturgical Press) and *We Send You Forth: Dismissals for the RCIA* by Jerry Galipeau (WLP/GIA).

Resources

Ammerman, Nancy T., Jackson W. Carroll, Carl S. Dudley, William McKinney. *Studying Congregations: A New Handbook*. Nashville: Abingdon Press, 1998.

Anslinger, Leisa, Mary A. Ehle, Biagio Mazza, Victoria Tufano. *The Living Word: Leading RCIA Dismissals Years A, B, C*. Chicago: Liturgy Training Publications, 2017, 2018, 2019.

Baima, Thomas A., ed. *What Is a Parish? Canonical, Pastoral, and Theological Perspectives*. Chicago: Liturgy Training Publications, 2011.

Birmingham, Mary. *Year-Round Catechumenate*. Chicago: Liturgy Training Publications, 2003.

Boselli, Goffredo. *The Spiritual Meaning of the Liturgy: School of Prayer, Source of Life*. Translated by Barry Hudock. Collegeville, MN: Liturgical Press, 2014.

Cahalan, Kathleen A. *Introducing the Practice of Ministry*. Collegeville, MN: Liturgical Press, 2010.

Cantalamessa, Raniero. *Mary: Mirror of the Church*. Translated by Frances Lonergan Villa. Collegeville, MN: Liturgical Press, 1992.

Catechism of the Catholic Church. Washington, DC: United States Conference of Catholic Bishops, 1997.

Connors, Michael E. *Preaching for Discipleship: Preparing Homilies for Christian Initiation*. Chicago: Liturgy Training Publications, 2018.

DeGrocco, Joseph. *A Pastoral Commentary on the General Instruction of the Roman Missal*. Chicago: Liturgy Training Publications, 2011.

Duggan, Bob, Carol Gura, Rita Ferrone, Gael Gensler, Steve Lanza, Donna Steffen, Maureen Kelly. *Foundations in Faith*. Allen, TX: Resources for Christian Living, 1997–2010.

Dulles, Avery Cardinal. *Models of the Church*. New York: Doubleday, 2002.

Eschenauer, Donna M. *The Role of the Coordinator in Christian Initiation: A Pastoral and Practical Guide*. Chicago: Liturgy Training Publications, 2017.

———. "Shaping a Living, Active Faith." *Pastoral Liturgy* 47, no. 2 (March/April 2016): 21–23.

———. "The People of God and the *Rite of Christian Initiation of Adults*: Forming and Re-forming the Life of the Church." *Catechumenate: A Journal of Christian Initiation* 35, no. 5 (September 2013): 28–37.

———. "The Sacraments of Initiation: A Guiding Theme for the Future of Lay Ecclesial Ministry." In *Reflections on Renewal Lay Ecclesial Ministry and the Church*, edited by Donna M. Eschenauer and Harold Daly Horell, 114–124. Collegeville, MN: Liturgical Press, 2011.

Francis. *Gaudete et Exsultate*. Huntington, IN: Our Sunday Visitor, 2018.

———. *The Joy of Discipleship*. Chicago: Loyola Press, 2016.

———. *Evangelii gaudium*. Washington, DC: United States Conference of Catholic Bishops, 2013.

Furnish, Victor Paul. "Theology and Ministry in the Pauline Letters." In *A Biblical Basis for Ministry*, edited by Earl E. Shelp and Ronald Sunderland, 101–144. Philadelphia: The Westminster Press, 1982.

Gensler, Gael, Timothy A. Johnston, Corinna Laughlin, Kyle Lechtenberg. *Disciples Making Disciples: Print and Digital Resources for Forming the Assembly*. Chicago: Liturgy Training Publications, 2017.

Hahnenberg, Edward P. *Ministries: A Relational Approach*. New York: Crossroads, 2003.

———. *Awakening Vocation: A Theology of Christian Call*. Collegeville, MN: Liturgical Press, 2010.

———. *Theology of Ministry: An Introduction for Lay Ministries*. Collegeville, MN: Liturgical Press, 2014.

Hater, Robert J. *The Catholic Parish: Hope for a Changing World*. Mahwah, NJ: Paulist Press, 2004.

Harris, Maria. *Fashion Me a People: Curriculum in the Church*. Louisville: Westminster John Knox Press, 1989.

Harmless, William. *Augustine and the Catechumenate*. Rev. ed. Collegeville, MN: Liturgical Press, 2014.

Hiesberger, Jean Marie. *Fostering Leadership Skills in Ministry: A Parish Handbook*. Liguori, MO: Liguori Publications, 2008.

Huels, John M. *The Catechumenate and the Law: A Pastoral and Canonical Commentary for the Church in the United States*. Chicago: Liturgy Training Publications, 1994.

Irwin, Kevin. *Context and Text: Method in Liturgical Theology*. Rev. ed. Collegeville, MN: Liturgical Press, 2018.

Lewinski, Ronald. *Guide for Sponsors*. 4th ed. Chicago: Liturgy Training Publications, 2008.

———. *An Introduction to the RCIA: The Vision of Christian Initiation*. Chicago: Liturgy Training Publications, 2017.

John Paul II. *Christifideles laici*. 1988.

———. "*Ecclesia De Eucharistia*: On the Eucharist in Its Relationship to the Church." In *The Liturgy Documents: Volume One*, 229–260. Chicago: Liturgy Training Publications, 2012.

Mick, Lawrence E. *RCIA: Renewing the Church as an Initiating Assembly*. Collegeville, MN: Liturgical Press, 1989.

O'Connell Killen, and John DeBeer. *The Art of Theological Refection*. New York: The Crossroad Publishing Company, 1994.

O'Malley, Timothy P. *Divine Blessing: Liturgical Formation in the RCIA*. Collegeville, MN: Liturgical Press, 2019.

O'Meara, Thomas F. *Theology of Ministry*. New York: Paulist Press, 1999.

Ostdiek, Gilbert. *Mystagogy of the Eucharist: A Resource for Faith Formation*. Collegeville, MN: Liturgical Press, 2015.

Pauley, James C. *Liturgical Catechesis in the 21st Century: A School of Discipleship*. Chicago: Liturgy Training Publications, 2017.

Pohl, Christine D. *Making Room: Recovering Hospitality as a Christian Tradition*. Grand Rapids: William B. Eerdmans Publishing Company, 1999.

Ruzicki, Michael. *Guide for Training Initiation Ministers: An Introduction to the RCIA*. Chicago: Liturgy Training Publications, 2017.

Ruzicki, Michael, Victoria Tufano, D. Todd Williamson, and Terry Navarro. *Signs and Symbols of the Liturgy: An Experience of Ritual and Catechesis*. Chicago: Liturgy Training Publications, 2018.

Sanford, John A. *Ministry Burnout*. New York: Paulist Press, 1982.

Second Vatican Council. "*Ad gentes*." In *Vatican II: The Basic Sixteen Documents; Constitutions, Decrees, Declarations*, edited by Austin Flannery. Collegeville, MN: Liturgical Press, 2014. First published in 1996 by Dominican Publications.

———. "*Christus Dominus*." In *Vatican II: The Basic Sixteen Documents; Constitutions, Decrees, Declarations*, edited by Austin Flannery. Collegeville, MN: Liturgical Press, 2014. First published in 1996 by Dominican Publications.

———. "*Lumen Gentium*." In *Vatican II: The Basic Sixteen Documents; Constitutions, Decrees, Declarations*, edited by Austin Flannery. Collegeville, MN: Liturgical Press, 2014. First published in 1996 by Dominican Publications.

———. "*Sacrosanctum concilium*." In *Vatican II: The Basic Sixteen Documents; Constitutions, Decrees, Declarations*, edited by Austin Flannery. Collegeville, MN: Liturgical Press, 2014. First published in 1996 by Dominican Publications.

Senseman, Rita Burns, Victoria Tufano, D. Todd Williamson. *Guide for Celebrating Christian Initiation of Adults with Children*. Chicago: Liturgy Training Publications, 2017.

Shelp, Earl E., and Ronald Sunderland, eds. *A Biblical Basis for Ministry*. Philadelphia: The Westminster Press, 1982.

Sofield, S.T. Loughlan, and Donald H. Kuhn. *The Collaborative Leader: Listening to the Wisdom of God's People*. Notre Dame, IN: Ave Maria Press, 1995.

Steffen, Donna. *Discernment in Christian Initiation*. Chicago: Liturgy Training Publications, 2018.

Stice, Randy. *Understanding the Sacraments of Initiation: A Rite-Based Approach*. Chicago: Liturgy Training Publications, 2017.

Sutton, Barbara. *Seeing the Word: Program Manual*. Collegeville, MN: Liturgical Press, 2011.

Seeing the Word *is a program of guided reflection that makes it possible to pray with images from* The Saint John's Bible. *It is a helpful resource for team development as well as a prayer and catechetical tool for those in the initiation process. Visit www.seeingtheword.org for more information and resources.*

The Liturgy Documents. Volume 1, 2, 3. Chicago: Liturgy Training Publications, 2012.

The Catechetical Documents: A Parish Resource. Chicago: Liturgy Training Publications, 1996.

Tufano, Victoria M. *Disciples Making Disciples: The Role of the Assembly in Christian Initiation*. Chicago: Liturgy Training Publications, 2017.

Tufano, Victoria M., Paul Turner, D. Todd Williamson. *Guide for Christian Initiation with Adults*. Chicago: Liturgy Training Publications, 2017.

Turner, Paul. *Q&A on the RCIA: A Guide to Understanding Christian Initiation*. Chicago: Liturgy Training Publications, 2019.

———. *The Hallelujah Highway: A History of the Catechumenate*. Chicago: Liturgy Training Publications, 2000.

———. *Ages of Initiation: The First Two Christian Millennia*. Collegeville, MN: Liturgical Press, 2000.

Tuzik, Robert L., ed. *How Firm a Foundation: Leaders of the Liturgical Movement*. Chicago: Liturgy Training Publications, 1990.

USCCB. *The Order of Confirmation*. Washington, DC: United States Conference of Catholic Bishops, 2016.

———. *Building Intercultural Competence for Ministers*. Washington, DC: United States Conference of Catholic Bishops, 2011.

———. *Go and Make Disciples: A National Plan and Strategy for Catholic Evangelization in the United States*. Washington, DC: United States Conference of Catholic Bishops, 2002.

———. *Welcoming the Stranger Among Us: Unity in Diversity*. Washington, DC: United States Conference of Catholic Bishops, 2000.

———. *Our Hearts Were Burning within Us: A Pastoral Plan for Adult Faith Formation in the United States*. Washington, DC: United States Conference of Catholic Bishops, 1999.

———. *Go and Make Disciples: A National Plan and Strategy for Catholic Evangelization in the United States*. Washington, DC: United States Conference of Catholic Bishops, 2002.

———. *The General Instruction of the Roman Missal*. Washington, DC: United States Conference of Catholic Bishops, 2011.

———. *Program of Priestly Formation*. 5th ed. Washington, DC: United States Conference of Catholic Bishops, 2006.

———. *National Directory for Catechesis*. Washington, DC: United States Conference of Catholic Bishops, 2005.

———. *Co-Workers in the Vineyard of the Lord: A Resource for Guiding the Development of Lay Ecclesial Ministry*. Washington, DC: United States Conference of Catholic Bishops, 2005.

———. *National Directory for the Formation, Ministry, and Life of Permanent Deacons*. Washington, DC: United States Conference of Catholic Bishops, 2005.

Walsh, Liam G. *Sacraments of Initiation: A Theology of Rite, Word, and Life*. Chicago: Liturgy Training Publications, 2011.

Weddell, Sherry A. *Forming Intentional Disciples: The Path to Knowing and Following Jesus*. Huntington, IN: Our Sunday Visitor, 2012.

Willimon, William H. *Clergy and Laity Burnout*. Nashville, TN: Abingdon Press, 1989.

Wittberg, Patricia. *Catholic Cultures: How Parishes Can Respond to the Changing Face of Catholicism*. Collegeville, MN: Liturgical Press, 2016.

Wilbright, Stephen S. *The Role of the Priest in Christian Initiation*. Chicago: Liturgy Training Publications, 2017.

Yarnold, Edward. *The Awe-Inspiring Rites of Initiation: The Origins of the RCIA*. Collegeville, MN: Liturgical Press, 1994.